KASHMIRI PROVERBS

Volume II

Koshur Kahawat	कांशिर्य कहावत	کوشر کھاوت
Koshur Muhavare	कांशिर्य मुहावरे	کوشر محاورے
Kashmiri Dapit	कांशिर्य दपित	کوشر دپیت

DR. RAJ KACHRU

INDIA · SINGAPORE · MALAYSIA

Copyright © Dr. Raj Kachru 2022
All Rights Reserved.

ISBN 979-8-88805-405-5

This book has been published with all efforts taken to make the material error-free after the consent of the author. However, the author and the publisher do not assume and hereby disclaim any liability to any party for any loss, damage, or disruption caused by errors or omissions, whether such errors or omissions result from negligence, accident, or any other cause.

While every effort has been made to avoid any mistake or omission, this publication is being sold on the condition and understanding that neither the author nor the publishers or printers would be liable in any manner to any person by reason of any mistake or omission in this publication or for any action taken or omitted to be taken or advice rendered or accepted on the basis of this work. For any defect in printing or binding the publishers will be liable only to replace the defective copy by another copy of this work then available.

Background picture of the cover: 'Kashmir paper mache' artwork on a wooden divider screen at Kashmir Museum, Srinagar. (Photo by R Ramani)

Dedicated to...

*The Goddess Jagdamba Sharika Bhagawati (an incarnation of Mata
Durga/Shakti), Hari Parvat, Srinagar, Kashmir (J&K) and
my grandparents...*

Smt. Veshmal (Ded) and Pt. Srikanth Kachru (Babuji) and parents...

*Smt. Gunwati (Kika) and Pt. Prem Nath Kachru (Maam),
real time Karmyogi!*

Contents

A

C

D

H

I

J

K

L

M

Maaje Gabur Aasun
माजि गबुर आसुन 144

Meder Mekraaz
मदुर म्यकुराज़ 145

Mia-nyan Kathan Chho-che' Karini
म्यान्यन कथन च्वचि करनि 146

Mordas Chhih Wadaan Bihit, Batas Chhih Wadaan Wudanih
मोरदस छि‍ वदान बिहित, बतस छि‍ वदान वोदनी 147

Mot Lagith Saale Batta Khyon
मोत लांगिथ सालु बतु ख्योन 149

Mugal Dishit Gatshih Pharsi Khasuni
मौगल डीशित गछि‍ फॉरसी खुसुन 150

Mulan Drot Tah Patran Sag
मूलन द्रोत तु पुत्रन सग 151

Myani Gurea Ne Leadh Laaer
मयानि गुरि नु लय्दु लय‍ुर 153

N

Naagah Gaadah, Wuchhanih Halaal Tah Khenih Haraam
नागु गाड़, वुछनि हलहल तु ख्यनि हराम 154

Naar Dhrav Souun Aasun
नारु द्राव स्वन आसुन 156

Nah Gamih Dozakh, Nah Gamih Jannat
नॉ गमि दोज़ख, नॉ गमि जन्नथ 157

Nam Ai Wuthih Tah Maazas Dag, Maaz Ai Wuthih Tah Namas Dag
नम हय व्वथि तु माज़स दग, माज़ हय व्वथि तु नमस दग 158

T

U

V

Contents

W

X

Foreword

The beginnings of my association with Dr. Raj Kachru goes back several decades, but then it was purely professional. With the passage of time, we continued to interact with each other in areas of common interest. I always found him pursuing the assignments he undertakes with passion; his zeal has remained undiminished with age.

Kashmiri is a spoken language of Kashmir valley with Dardic origins and elements of Indian languages. It is estimated that about 10 million people understand or speak Kashmiri around the world. Documentation of spoken wisdom is imperative; otherwise, time will erase it from our memories and the society. Kashmiri Proverbs Vol 2 by Dr. Raj Kachru, (a sequel to Vol 1 by the same name) should therefore be viewed as a service to Kashmiri language, one of the oldest spoken languages of the Indian subcontinent.

Covid-19 pandemic has made a tremendous impact on people's lives globally in various spheres. Forced confinement at home turned several people restless, making them venture into new initiatives. The pandemic seems to have turned Dr. Kachru into a paremiologist; he started writing Kashmiri Proverbs with their English meanings and explanations, one at a time, and shared them through social networks. They were not very different from the ones you will find in this volume as well as the previous one. The seeds were sown for the Vol 1 of Kashmiri Proverbs.

Proverbs are like spices to a food; they not only add style and flavour to speech but also help in reinforcing moral values; pacify or inspire the listeners. Going through the book, one will recognize the author's deep understanding of the language and the land. The way he relates various expressions to the habits, culture and beliefs of the Kashmiri people adds authenticity to the explanatory notes. He has added the proverbs in Devanagari and Urdu scripts to facilitate the readers to get the pronunciation and thus the right meaning. One might find some of the expressions sexist, but they should be understood in the context of the prevailing culture and beliefs of the land.

The readers might find similarity of some of the proverbs with those of their regions, in this country or elsewhere. This makes one identify with the Kashmiris. The author himself has cited several Western proverbs with parallel meanings. I could also relate several proverbs with those of Tamil Nadu. I share two of them:

Kashmiri Proverb 130: 'Shistarah Chhuh Shishtaras Tchataan.' – 'Iron is cut by iron'.

Tamil Equivalent: '*முள்ளை முள்ளால்தான் எடுக்க வேண்டும்*', which means 'We have to use a thorn to remove a thorn'.

Kashmiri Proverb 150: 'Zouvee Hindh Baapat Chhe Zett Naale Kadaan?' – For the sake of lice, garment is not removed from the body.

Tamil equivalent: '*செருப்புக்காகக் காலைத் தறிக்கிறதா?*' – Do you chop off the foot for the sake of the sandals?

I am sure that other readers, across diverse continents and cultures would also feel the same way.

At the same time, a non-native reader may find it difficult to fully comprehend the meaning of some of the proverbs as certain expressions in them can be understood only by the native speakers of Kashmiri.

I am extremely delighted to write the Foreword for this painstakingly compiled second volume of Kashmiri proverbs and expressions by Dr. Raj Kachru. India is a symbol of unity amidst diversity of cultures, languages and religions. The thought of a native Tamil speaker from the Southern-most state of the country writing the Foreword for a book on Kashmiri adages, spoken in the Northern-most part, brings a smile to my face.

The way in which each of the proverbs is elaborated makes this book stand apart from similar compilations of the past. The readers may also be tempted to come up with their own perception of the proverbs, based on the individual word meanings provided by the author.

I am sure every reader would find the book engrossing, like I did!

Dr. Ranganathan Ramani
Fmr. Director, ICAR-IINRG, Ranchi

Preface

The first volume of 'Kashmiri Proverbs', published in May 2021 was conceptualised and written during the coronavirus pandemic in 2020-21. Since then, I have received overwhelming response and feedback from the readers all over the world, especially Kashmiri diaspora from USA, UK and New Zealand.

The reviews and comments made by most of them on the book were very encouraging and appreciative. Some even suggested bringing out a second volume, containing new proverbs with improved interpretation and usage.

Here I need to make a mention that my respected eldest cousin (Shri Bansi Lal Kachru), being a teacher himself, apart from forwarding a few dozens of new proverbs, was most critical, mainly on the deficiencies found in the Devanagari (Hindi) part which have since been taken care of in this second volume. This was made possible by seeking assistance of a well-respected Kashmiri and Hindi-knowing teacher Smt. Karuna Raina presently based in New Zealand.

As already covered under the Preface of the first volume, proverbs are pithy statements, mostly derived from wisdom that expresses traditionally held truths or pieces of advice based on common sense or experience. The beauty of proverbs lies in fact that they hold true for all times, are well thought out and honed by our ancestors from time immemorial. Their popular usage in colloquial language and in 'Kashmiri' needs no emphasis! Proverbs may well be seen as 'spicy jargon' of Kashmiri language. Some may prefer to call a proverb a 'phrase', a 'saying', an 'adage', a 'maxim', or a 'catch phrase'. Proverbs use figurative language to make a statement that best encapsulates a society's values and beliefs. In fact, proverbs sometimes reveal truths about the culture of a society and the country more than any text book!

During this entire exercise, right from the conception of the idea of writing this book till date, I had to depend mostly on my senior Kashmiri friend, Prof. Chaman Lal Wakhaloo, a well-read man, knowledgeable in Kashmir history and language, particularly proverbs, for his valued guidance and continued encouragement.

Just naming Kashmiri proverbs may not be so difficult as to decipher the meaning of each word and its interpretation and usage. The mother of Kashmiri proverbs being Sanskrit, have absorbed over the years, words and phrases from almost all languages of the of the Asian Continent.

Surprisingly, I found two of my dear non-Kashmiri friends, one from Kerala, Dr. Krishna Iyer and the other from Tamil Nadu, Dr. Ranganathan Ramani, who have immensely helped me during the course of writing this volume.

The contributions and help rendered by both of them can be gone through in 'Acknowledgements' chapter of this book.

This compilation has 151 new proverbs each of which is scripted in English, Hindi and Urdu for wider reach and more importantly, to help the reader in pronouncing it rightly lest it should lead entirely to a different meaning and interpretation.

I have tried to translate each word of the proverb so as to offer the closest meaning though in some cases, it was impossible to give precise literal meaning.

For the information and benefit of readers, I have appended the 'Foreword', 'Preface', 'Acknowledgements' and a 'List of corrected Devanagari (Hindi) version of Proverbs of the 1st volume' with this volume for ready reference.

I hope these new proverbs would definitely evoke once again interesting memories in my Kashmiri brethren and would receive good reception from those of other regions using different languages.

I would appreciate receiving feedback and comments from the readers for enriching and improving my own understanding of these proverbs.

Thanks!   **Dr. Raj Kachru**

Acknowledgements

A number of incredibly thoughtful and supportive people have helped at various stages in identification, compilation of 151 new proverbs and deciphering them in a meaningful interpretation and usage.

To start off, I'm greatly indebted to my grandparents, Smt. Veshmal and Pt. Srikanth Kachru (a highly disciplined, spiritual and multilingual penman). Next, my parents, Smt. Gunwati and Pt. Prem Nath Kachru (a real time Karamyogi) for their upbringing, love and blessings. They instilled moral education too!

I express my sincere thanks to my family more so my wife, Madhu for her moral support, motivation and encouragement.

I'm greatly indebted to my respected eldest cousin, Shri. Bansi Lal Kachru, whose encouragement, constructive criticism also suggestions have immensely improved the quality of this volume more so, the Devanagari part of these proverbs. Further also identifying a few dozen new proverbs.

I'm highly obliged to my dear senior friend, Prof. Chaman Lal Wakhaloo, a renowned and well-read professor in Engineering Science, the founder Principal of Govt. Engineering College, Bhopal, that has since blossomed into Rajiv Gandhi Proudyogiki Vishwavidyalaya, Bhopal (Madhya Pradesh). He has been involved right from the day one in identifying additional new proverbs and their meanings and usage. In fact, I have yet to come across a Kashmiri who knows so much about history of Kashmir, her language and culture besides, remembering so many proverbs and their meaning. Earlier, he went through the first volume and wrote the 'Foreword'.

By share good luck, I came a across a well-respected Kashmiri knowing teacher, Smt. Karuna Raina (maiden name, Guddi Sahab), presently based in New Zealand. She painstakingly corrected the Devanagari (Hindi) version of all the 151 proverbs contained in this book, also corrected 101 proverbs covered in the first volume. She has been involved in many activities of the promotion of Kashmiri language and culture.

I express deep and sincere gratitude to my ex-colleagues and friends, Dr. Krishna Iyer and Dr. Ranganathan Ramani, former Directors, ICAR-CIRCOT, Mumbai and ICAR-IINRG, Ranchi, respectively for rendering great help in the preparation of the manuscript. Both being non-Kashmiri, surprised me more for their understanding and interest shown in these proverbs. The former has helped in editing the usage/interpretation of a good number of proverbs. Whereas, Dr. Ramani has been all the way helpful not only in this volume but, in the first volume, also in some other projects, I have been working from time to time. Dr. Ramani was kind enough to go through the manuscript of this volume and write a Foreword. He has always been there and ready as and when needed. No words of appreciation will be sufficient to describe his contribution here. Thanks a lot, Dr. Ramani for your selfless help!

I'm feeling short of words to express my sincere thanks to all those who have directly and indirectly helped to the run-up of this publication.

Dr. Raj Kachru

Kashmiri Proverb # 01

AAB TAL SHRAKH

आब् तल् श्राख

آب تل شراق

Meaning: AAB = Water

TAL = Under/In

SHRAAKH = Dagger.

A dagger under water.

Usage: A deceitful person stacks weapons like the knife, sword, chopper, dagger, etc., hidden in places where they are least expected to be spotted so that he could use them against his adversaries when they are off guard. The reference here is to a cunning, ruthless and vengeful, yet profoundly shrewd person who plots to assault and even eliminate his foes without much effort since he has arranged to keep the required assault weapons concealed from the view of prospective victims but within his easy reach.

History and legends are replete with episodes of the use of stealth weapons against adversaries. Afzal Khan's death at the hands of Shivaji and the killing of Bali by Rama stand testimony to the deft use of concealed weapons and deceitful ways of eliminating adversaries. Legitimacy or otherwise of such acts will, however, remain a matter of debate forever!

Kashmiri Proverb # 02

AASMAANAS LAAYENI THOUKH

आसमानस लायिन्य थ्वख

آسمانس لائینی تھوک

Meaning: AASMAANAS = Sky

LAAYENI = Throw at

THOUKH = Spit.

To spit at the sky.

Usage: The statement implies that if one tries to spit into the depths of the sky towards its zenith, the law of gravity ensures that the material would land directly upon the face of the one who attempted this act, in short the doer. It is the less capable people who harbour jealousy against the successful ones.

In practical life, it tells that if any one disrespects the elders, superiors and reverential persons, it would definitely result in self disgrace. So, one should desist from using a language or act to show someone down. It could boomerang back at you!

Kashmiri Proverb # 03

AASUN CHHU HAECHHINAAWAAN, NA AASUN CHHU MANDICHAAWAAN

आसुन छु हेछि नावान,
न आसुन छु मंदुछावान

آسون چھو ہیچھناوان،
نہ آسون چھو منديچھاوان

Meaning: AASUN = Property/Wealth

CHHU = Having

HAECHHINAAWAAN = Teaches

NA AASUN = Poverty/Not having wealth/property

MANDICHHAAWAAN = To shame.

Property/wealth teaches one, whereas poverty puts one to shame.

Usage: This proverb distinguishes between the haves and the have-nots, relates to their economic well-being and the consequences or the effects thereof.

Once the economic status improves, one gets recognition/respect in the society by getting lifted into the higher social circle/class. They adopt matching habits and mannerisms to get accommodated therein.

In case, the opposite situation occurs, one gets into a down-slide mode to find his/her feet/pedestal!

In other words, 'haves' teach you to learn and prosper but, 'have-nots' make you feel guilty and ashamed or prosperity improves one's personality while as adversity cripples it. Goswami Tulsidas has also said in his Doha, 'नहिं दरिद्र सम दुख जग माहीं!' अर्थात, गरीबी से बड़ा दुख या अभिशाप इस संसार मे नही है!, Or, 'There is no curse worse than poverty in this world!'

Kashmiri Proverb # 04

AKH GAV JAANI YAAR,
BYAAKH GAV NAANI YAAR

अख गव जॉनी यार,
ब्याख गव नॉन्य यार

اخ گو جانی یار
بیاخ گو نانی یار

Meaning: AKH = One

GAV = Is

JAANI = True

YAAR = Friend

BYAAKH = Another

NAANI = Sharing bread.

One is a true friend, the other for (sharing) the bread.

Usage: It is an universal and time tested truth that one who stays with you through thick and thin qualifies a bosom friend ('jaani yaar'), the other happens to be a 'fair weather friend' who is there with you to derive some benefits out of the friendship!

There is a Persian saying with a similar meaning, 'yaar-i-jaan o yaar-i-nan'

(یار - ی- جان او یار-ی- نان)

'Nan' or 'Naan', here in Persian means bread. The person becomes a friend only when he/she would like to get a share of the bread (here, meaning wealth, booty, etc.). One must therefore, differentiate between a true and a selfish friend!

34

Kashmiri Proverb # 05

AKH ZANANAH TSHHAI HATTH LANJEH' BOOEN, BYAAKH TSHHAI BARR-TAL HOONI-HISH

अख ज़नानॖ छे हथ लन्जि बून्य,
ब्याख छे बरॖ-तलॖ हून्य-हिश

اخ زنانه چھٕیہ ہتھ لنجھی بوئن،
بیاخ چھٕیہ برتل ہونیٕیش

Meaning: AKH = One

ZANANAH = Woman

TSHHAI = Is

HATTH = Hundred

LANJEH' = Branches

BOOEN = Chinar Tree*

BYAAKH = Another

BARR-TAL = At the door

HOONI-HISH = Like Bitch.

*BOOE'N/Chinar (*Platanus orientalis*) is the most popular and shade giving tree, introduced by Moghuls in Kashmir from Persia (Iran).

A lady could either be like a Chinar tree with hundreds of branches or like a bitch at the door.

Usage: It is said: Zan (woman), Zar (money) and Zamin (landed property) are all important, and any one of them can either make or mar one's life. A woman in the family, whether a mother or a wife, has a key role to play in bringing up the children and maintaining cordial relationship with the members of the entire household and of the neighbourhood. She is likened to an expansive Chinar tree – she protects and cares for her family like the Chinar which provides shade, shelter and solace to those who take refuge. Antithesis to this gracious lady can also be seen in abundance in families and segments of society. Articulations and actions of such women may bring disharmony among people all around. The proverb equates these elements to female canines stationed as sentinels at residential gates. One finds such type of women in every society.

Kashmiri Proverb # 06

AKHA GOMUT AANTE (YEERE'), VEERI MANGAAN TANGG

अखाह गोमुत आन्तु (यीरु), वीरि मंगान टन्ग

اخا گوموت آنتہ(ییری)،ویری منگان ٹنگ

Meaning: AKHA = A person

GOMUT = Gone

AANTE = Gullible/Simpleton

YEERE' = Sailing with the current of water flow

VEERI = Willow tree

MANGAAN = Asks

TANGG = Pear Fruit.

A person has turned so gullible to seek a pear fruit from a willow tree.

Usage: There are occasions in life when one gets trapped in a helpless situation such as being carried away by a water current, even as he hopes against hope, to be saved by a good Samaritan. As in the English proverb about a drowning man clutching even a straw, this man too will try all means, practicable or infeasible, logical or irrational, to avert a catastrophe. In his desperation and anxiety, he may hope to be saved by a miracle in the same manner as one could ask for and get a pear fruit from a willow tree!

Kashmiri Proverb # 07

AKIS CHHE' DAZAAN DAE'R TE' BYAAK CHHUS WUSHANAAWAAN ATHA

अकिस छि दज़ान दॉर तु बयाख छुस वुशनावान अथु

اکیس چھ دزان دیر تہ بیاک چھوس وُشناوان اتھ

Meaning: AKIS = One

CHHE' = Is

DAZAAN = On fire

DAE'R = Beard

TE' = And

BYAAK = Another

CHHUS = Is

WUSHANAAWAAN = Warms

ATHA = Hands.

One person's beard is on fire and the another person is warming his hands with it.

Usage: This proverb uses the metaphor of a man's beard catching fire while others merrily warm their palms, to illustrate a familiar social experience of someone facing difficulty while others, instead of coming forward to his rescue, rejoice and exploit his discomfiture, for their own benefit and pleasure. Such people who gleefully perform what in effect is 'fishing in troubled waters', are insensitive to the pain endured by the affected person, but they do derive immense sadistic pleasure. Such people may not be delighted so much by their own success as by the distress caused to the other person! Human society has an abundance of such people.

Kashmiri Proverb # 08

AMIS CHHAI MYAVAS KUN ZAN PATCHHI

अमिस छैय म्यवस कुन ज़न पचि

امس چھے میوس کون زن پہچھی

Meaning: AMIS = He/She

CHHAI = Has

MYAVAS = Fruits

KUN = Towards

ZAN = Like

PATCHHI = Wooden Planks.

He/She appears to be averse to eating fruits as if there is a barrier of wooden planks.

Usage: Young children and adolescents of today have little affinity or appetite for healthy foods like fruits and greens, but they do crave for junk eatables that are readily available all over the market place. Most of these food items may entice them with aroma, appearance and flavour, but in the long run have adverse effects on the overall health of a person.

To a greater extent, the responsibility rests with the parents to inculcate good eating habits in their children right from the beginning and not to pamper them by yielding to their demands.

Kashmiri Proverb # 09

ANDHRAMMAN HAEMMAS SHUMAAR

अन्द्रमन ह्यमस शुमार

اندرمن ہیمس شُمار

Meaning: ANDHRAMMAN = Intestines

HAEMMAS = Will/Can

SHUMAAR = Count.

Will/can count one's intestines.

Usage: Counting the intestines may sound absurd in as much as there are only two types of them in every human being. Nevertheless the proverb gains attention through its veiled message that a clever and learned person can thoroughly read another's mind. He can visualise what the other man is up to or whether he/she is facing problems. The fall guy can't hide and has no room for escaping the clever person's judgement about him/her. This kind of attribute in a person could be acquired through experience supported by an analytical mind. Ordinarily, one can't dodge or hoodwink this type of person for he would have known the victim's strengths and weaknesses alike.

Kashmiri Proverb # 10

ANIS HAAVAAN SARRI WATH BE-AKLAS NAH KANH

अनिस हावान सॉरी वथ, बे-अकलस न कांह

انیس ہاوان سري وتھ،بیکلاس نہ کہنہ

Meaning: ANIS = Blind

HAAVAAN = Show

SARRI = All

WATH = Way

BE-AKLAS = Person without understanding

NAH KANH = No body.

Everyone will be willing to guide the way to a blind person, but not to a stupid.

Usage: Blind and otherwise handicapped persons being guided and helped by good Samaritans on roads and in other public places is a familiar sight. A sense of benevolence and eagerness to reach out to persons with such inherent shortcomings would seem to be instinctive in human beings. But no one would come forward to help a person who is naive, hare-brained, unreceptive and unable to grasp anything.

Note: However, is the society justified in showing indifference to such luckless, disadvantaged people? After all, being born with handicaps is not their fault. Public perception about such unfortunate beings and people's attitude towards the hapless ones need a radical change.

Kashmiri Proverb # 11

ARI AI SARI TAH, UR GAV NAH KANH

अर्यआयि सॉरी तु, ऒर गव नु कान्ह

ار آئی سری ته،اور گوؤ نه کنه

Meaning:

ARI = Healthy

AI = Came

SARI = All

THE = But

UR = Healthy

GAV = Gone

NAH = No

KANH = Anyone.

Everyone arrived healthy, but none returned healthy.

Usage: All are born healthy and live healthy until ill-health drives them to death. That is the law of nature. What one can, and must do, is to prolong life through a healthy regime of feed, work and repose. As long as one stays healthy, death will have no choice but to wait at the door. However, one can't expect to leave this world in the same healthy condition as when born!

Kashmiri Proverb # 12

ASHRAF GAV SUI, YAS ASHRAFI AASIH

अशरफ गव सुइ, यस अशर्फुआसि

اشرف گاؤ سوی،یس اشرفی آسیہ

Meaning: ASHRAF = Honorable

GAV = Will be

SUI = Who

YAS = Who

ASHRAFI = Sovereigns

AASIH = Possesses.

Honour is bestowed upon those who possess sovereigns (wealth).

Usage: A person is accorded respect if he/she is rich. Here, richness denotes not only material wealth but also human values like compassion, honesty, humility, helpfulness, etc., all of which evoke respectful response from family and society.

If he loses the above assets, the respect will fade. One is reminded of a legend in which a rich man who commanded respect found people indifferent after he lost all wealth. When queried by him, the village Chieftain clarified: 'people respected not you but Goddess Lakshmi who was with you then'. Values are respected, not the possessor!

Kashmiri Proverb # 13

ASMAANAS SEITH BUEZ BUEZ GAADI KHENI

असमानस सुत्य बुज़्य बुज़्य गाड़ खेनि

آسمانس سیت بیوز بیوز گاڑھی خیني

Meaning: ASMAANAS = Sky

SEITH = On

BUEZ = To roast

GAADI = Fishes

KHENI = To eat.

To roast fishes on sky and eat them.

Usage: The proverb states that the man cooks his fish by the sun and eats. The person is full of him/her self, that he/she listens to nobody. Such people think too much of themselves and always boast and feel proud to know everything. Often, these ones are timid possessing shallow bent of mind. One could even qualify these ones as saucy. Also, they believe to live on a fake prestige.

Kashmiri Proverb # 14

ATHA-CHAN PAANCCHAN UNGAJAN MANZ KIS LOUKUT, MUHR CCHIH MELAAN KISI

अथुचन पांचुन उंगजुन मंज़ किस लकुट, मोह छु मेलान किसि

اتهچن پانچن اونگگجن مِہنز کِس لوکوٹ، محر چّھ میلان کیسہ

Meaning: ATHA-CHAN = Hand's

PAANCCHAN = Out of five

UNGAJAN = Fingers

MANZ = In

KIS = Little finger

LOUKUT = Smallest

MUHR = Signet ring

CCHI = Is

MELAAN = Given

KISI = Little finger.

Of the five fingers of a hand, the signet ring decorates the smallest one (little finger).

Usage: In the world around us, we find people with different levels of strengths and weaknesses, making the society truly heterogeneous in character. Each one of them would have the potential to perform well in a handful of tasks. One should never underrate or trivialise the capacity and calibre of any of them merely based on appearance which at times can be monumentally deceptive. It is not uncommon to encounter self-effacing persons performing better than others and winning laurels and recognition. It is but aptly said, the humble shall be exalted.

Kashmiri Proverb # 15

AZAR VANIS NAZAR BAND

अज़र व़निस नज़र बन्द

عذر وينس نظر بند

Meaning: AZAR = Jealous/Envious

VANIS = One

NAZAR BAND = Sight shut off/Become blind.

Let jealous people go blind.

Usage: Jealousy is an emotion that makes people wish that they do not see anything good happening to others. It is as if they prefer to be blind rather than be forced to view the greatness attributed to others.

Jealousy sprouts in a person because of low self-esteem, lack of confidence in himself and a general feeling of insecurity. This ignoble mental state is destined to outlive the joy of those who happen to be the objects of envy.

Jealousy is a debilitating psycho-pathological disorder. It will hold back the 'patient' from enjoying happiness. It is wisely said, the jealous die not once, but as often as those envied keep winning accolades!

B

Kashmiri Proverb # 16

BAR DITH KHAR NATSUN

बर दिथ खर नच्चुन

بر ڈیتھ خر نچھون

Meaning: BAR = Door

DITH = Closed

KHAR = Donkey/Ass

NATSUN = Dancing.

An ass dances behind shut doors.

Usage: The proverb is a Kashmiri 'prattle', which states that a donkey is dancing behind closed doors. The answer of this riddle/prattle is, a hand operated pair of (round) millstones used for grinding grains. These millstones were in vogue before the advent of machine age!

The proverb could be used for people who happen to be highly spirited and verbose within the four walls of their home, but once outside in public prefer to keep their counsel.

Kashmiri Proverb # 17

BATAH NA TE BATAAS, CHHOCHHI NA TE LAVAAS

बतᵘ नᵊ तᵊ बतासᵘ, छᵥचᵘ नᵊ तᵊ लवासᵘ

بتھ نہ تہ بتاس،چوچھ نہ تہ لواس

Meaning:

BATAH = Rice/Food

NA = Not

TE = Having

BATAAS[1] = Sweets

CHHOCHHI[2] = Bread (Chapati)

LAVAAS[3] = A bread.

[1] White sugar candy.

[2] Earthen oven baked ordinary (circular) bread.

[3] Earthen oven baked special, thin and circular bread.

No food in the house, yet wishes to have sugar candies, no simple bread in the house, yet wishes to have special bread.

Usage: The proverb states that a person cannot afford a simple square meal yet dreams/yearns to eat exotic/special dishes. Instead of plain rice, fancies sugar candies and instead of simple bread, would like to have special loaves of bread.

The poor man is having great desires.

There is a similar proverb in Kashmir, 'Batah nah tah bataas, chhit nah tah saatan!'

Chhit (छिठ) or Chintz (in UK) here means a cheap rough ragged cloth (printed with flowers) and saatan (साटन) means satin (costly refined cloth).The guy does not have even rice at home, yet desires to have sweet candy and does not even have a ragged cloth to his back, yet he wishes for satin.

One should avoid to have a desire, which is beyond one's reach.

Kashmiri Proverb # 18

BATTAH GAV GRATTAH

बट् गव ग्रट्

بٹہ گوو گرٹھ

Meaning: BATTAH[1] = Kashmiri Pandit

GAV = Is

GRATTAH[2] = Millstone/Mill

[1]A term, reserved especially, for qualifying a Kashmiri Pandit. Female, is called as 'BATTIN'.

[2] Conventional equipment made of two circular pieces of granite stones used for milling grains, manually.

Battah (Kashmiri Pandit) is a stone mill*.

Usage: Muslims and others in Kashmir, jestingly refer to a Pandit (Battah) as 'Mill Stone'. By his/her very nature, a frugal/simple/unassuming person, yet careful and sensitive about self-respect, a Pandit takes time to open up.

These inherent characteristics of a 'Battah' are a reflection of an effort not to receive a reprimand or be labelled as a slipshod, but be seen as thorough in his/her work/assignment. Besides, a mill stone grinds every grain and hence is a hard task master for self and also for others. 'Grattah' metaphor is perhaps justified.

Kashmiri Proverb # 19

BATTAH PAAWIH TAL CHHE AIBAH KHAAR GAEB

बतॣ पावि तल छि ऑबॣ खार गॉब

بتّہ پاویہ تل چھ ائبہ خار غیب

Meaning: BATTAH = Rice

PAAWIH[1] = Unit of weight

TAL = Under/Beneath

CHHE = Is

AIBAH = Shortcoming

KHAAR[2] = Unit of weight

GAEB = Concealed/Lost.

[1] Paaw, is 1/4th part of one Kilogram = 250 grams

[2] One Khaar = 16 Trakh

One Trakh = 4.43 Kilogram.

Beneath a Paaw of rice, a Khaar of drawbacks is concealed.

Usage: Most people like to conceal their weaknesses, blemishes and vices by means of cleverly-crafted camouflages so as to appear acceptable in society and be not looked down upon.

It is particularly so with people holding undeserving wealth gathered by sinful means. To cover up the sins and multitudes of wrong doings, they have to find alibis and in the process, commit more of such transgressions. The irony of life, however, is that the riches thus earned have the potential to shut off the wrong doings from the eyes of the society; and the players are able to move about as clean and honest gentlemen.

Kashmiri Proverb # 20

BE-KAARAS CHHI TREH KAAR

बेकारस छि त्रे कार

بیکار چھے ترہ کار

Meaning: BE-KAAR = Idle

CHHI = Having

TREH = Three

KAAR = Works.

An idle person has only three tasks.

Usage: For an idle person, there are only three things to perform in a day's routine: eat to satiate, engage in squabbles and enjoy siesta. As the adage goes, an idle mind is the devil's workshop. A mind with no space to contemplate doing anything constructive, has ample room to harbour evil and sinful thoughts. Abundance of leisure has the potential to let wicked thoughts enter our minds. Accepting the dictum 'Work is Worship' and keeping ourselves engaged mentally and physically at all times will be a healthy practice!

Kashmiri Proverb # 21

BE-SUNMB CHHUH DAPAAN, MEH SUNMB NAH KANH

बेसुम छु दपान, मेसुम न कांह

بھے-سونب چھو دپان، مہ سونمب نہ کھنہ

Meaning: BE-SUNMB = Unequal

CHHUH = Is

DAPAAN = Telling/Says

MEH = I

SUNMB = Equal

NAH KANH = Nobody.

The unequal man says, I haven't an equal.

Usage: It has often been observed that a well-up and upright person keeps a somber profile, reacts/transacts in a humble gentlemanly (womanly) style even if handled roughly. Whereas in comparison, a person not so well up or lowly placed, culturally or otherwise aggressive in his/her effort for parity exhibits a short tempered/apparently clever, sometimes irritant profile. One finds such people in all walks of life, viz, family, workplace, society, etc.

While as, the really great men and women think themselves less than the least. A similar quote by Ramakrishna carries the same meaning, 'the tree laden with fruits always bends low and if you wish to be great, be humble!

Finally, it is the humility which plays a significant role in each and every relationship!

Kashmiri Proverb # 22

BEYEH-SUND DOAD CHHUI BE-MAANE, YAMISEI GUDHRE SUI-ZAANE

बेयि सुन्द दोद छुय बे माने, यमिसुय गुदिरे सुय ज़ाने

بیہ-سوند دود چھوئی بیمانے ،یمسی گدرے سوی زانے

Meaning: BEYEH-SUND = Another's

DOAD = Pain

CHHUI = Is

BE-MAANE = Without meaning

YAMISEI = One who

GUDHRE = Suffers

SUI = He

ZAANE = Knows.

Another's pain is without meaning, only one who suffers, knows what it is like.

Usage: As said by George Herbert, 'it is only the wearer who knows where the shoe pinches'. A person directly afflicted by a bout of pain or unhappiness alone can perceive its severity. Everyone else is able to only stand by and sympathize. Moreover, only the person who faces trouble or difficulty will know its cause. A person whose belly always stays full can't understand what hunger is, just as it is impossible for any person to form the right judgement of his/her neighbour's suffering (Addison). The above proverb comes handy to describe such situations.

Kashmiri Proverb # 23

BOCHHE'-HATTIS, PHORRI PULAO

ब्वछि-हॅतिस, फोहरि प्वलाव

بوچھ ہتیس،فوحری پلاوٗ

Meaning: BOCHHE' – HATTIS = Hungry man

PHORRI* = Lacy/Crunchy layer that forms at the bottom of the rice cooking pot.

*Also called as 'Tahdig' in Persian-

PULAO = Casserole, a recipe of rice preparation (a delicacy) with stock or broth, spices, meat/vegetables, dry fruits, etc.

For a hungry man, bottom layer of the cooked rice is like a pulao.

Usage: When a person is hungry, he will relish the bottom layer of cooked rice in the pot. Whether the stuff is cold and stale, or warm and fresh, would not make a difference for him. It would all seem equally delectable. As they say, hunger is the sauce that can augment the taste of food.

Kashmiri Proverb # 24

BUTHIH PHUER AASUN

बुथ्य फ्युर आसुन

بوتھی پھویر آسون

Meaning: BUTHIH PHUER = One who replies bluntly

AASUN = Is.

One who replies bluntly.

Usage: Allusion here is to a person who is blunt, curt and bereft of courtesy in conversation with people. He would not care two hoots about the feelings of even elders, leave alone of juniors, while engaged in a chat. He would use the same rough language for expressing his views or replying to others. Maintaining propriety or politeness is not part of his demeanour. Society views him with disdain and wise men avoid speaking to him.

C

Kashmiri Proverb # 25

CHHALNI-I-MAL CHHA ATSAAN KINI NERAAN?

छलनु मल छा अच्चान किनु नेरान?

چھلنی مل چھااچآن کن نیران؟

Meaning: CHHALNI = Washing

MAL = Dirt

CHHA = Does

ATSAAN = Enters

KINI = Or

NERAAN = Removes.

Does the washing make clothes dirty or clean?

Usage: The proverb states that washing of clothes or any other item removes the dirt and does not make it more dirty. And, washing it repeatedly shall eventually remove all the dirt to make it clean.

It is advisable to discuss the problems with those concerned to sort out the differences and to find the right solutions.

This holds good between the communities, states, countries which are at loggerheads. They can resolve any contemptuous issues by a dialogue/talking to each other.

Kashmiri Proverb # 26

CHHOUNTH VOUTSHIT TSHU CHHOUNTH RUNG RATTAAN

चून्ठ वुछिथ छु, चून्ठ रंग रटान

چونٹھ وچّیت چھو چونٹھ رنگ رٹان

Meaning: CHHOUNTH = Apple

VOUTSHIT = By seeing

TSHU = Is

RUNG = Color

RATTAAN = Gets/Adopts.

The apple picks up its color by looking at other apples.

Usage: This proverb makes a hyperbolic claim that an unripe apple, if placed in a box of ripe ones will tend to attain the colour of the latter, and soon ripen too! The message carried by the proverb is that the environment influences a person's outlook, and appearance. Friendship with good people will, therefore, be rewarding for everyone. A man's character and behaviour are greatly swayed by external influences. As the saying goes, the man is known by the company he keeps. Friendship with a group of virtuous men will portray you as a good person. At the same time, in a deplorable company, you will be seen as a bad character even if individually you possess laudable qualities. Parents must ensure that their children cultivate friendship with only those endowed with good, moral character.

Kashmiri Proverb # 27

CHOUNTH (AEES) SURVITH* KATH KARYEN

चोन्ठ (ऑस) सुरवित कथ करुन्य

چونٹھ (ایس) سورویت کتھ کرین

Meaning: CHOUNTH/AEES = Mouth

SURVIT = Cleaned

KATH = Speak/Talk

KARYEN = Do.

Cleanse your mouth before you speak.

Usage: In olden times in Kashmir, especially during the winter when the water is ice-cold kitchen utensils were cleaned with ash referred to as 'Soor' left over in kitchen hearths that made use of fire-wood, charcoal or cow-dung cake.

*Survith, is derived from 'Soor' or Sur, defined above and 'Vith', meaning, 'with'.

Thus, meaning: cleaning with ash.

The proverb is used to mean that you must think before you open your mouth to speak, and be careful about what you are speaking.

Also, utter your words with utmost caution, keeping in mind whom you are speaking to.

Kashmiri Proverb # 28

DAANDAS CHHA HENG GOBAAN?

दांदस छा हॆंग गॊबान?

داندس چِھا ہینگ گوبان؟

Meaning: DAANDAS = Bullock

CHHA = Does/Are

HENG = Horns

GOBAAN = Feeling Heavy.

Are the horns too heavy for the bullock?

Usage: A bullock/bull never feels it's horns as burden for it. In general, animals have a variety of uses for horns and antlers, including defending themselves from predators and fighting members of their own species. Thus, it is an asset and not a burden. Similarly, a parent does not feel their offspring are a burden for them and a fruit tree never feels the load of its fruits. The proverb holds good also for the animal kingdom.

No matter, how large the family, the father would not willingly part with one of his children.

The head of the family, organization or State carry their responsibility/duty to look after each of its members/ employees equally without thinking them as burden at any point of time.

Kashmiri Proverb # 29

DAB LUG TAH RABI PEATH
DIL LUG TAH HILI PEATH

दब लोग, रबि प्यठ,
दिल लोग, हिलि प्यठ

دب لوگ تہ ربی پیٹھ،
دِل لوگ تہ ہلی پیٹھ

Meaning: DAB = Tumbled

LUG TAH = Into

RABI = Mud

DIL = Heart

HILI = Water weeds.

Tumbled into the mud, the heart sets upon water weeds.

Usage: The proverb literally means, 'once you fancy a water hyacinth (water weed) and in your effort to pick up and own it, one may slip on the muck'! Typical example is the one of Edward the VIII, King George the VI's elder brother, who fancied a widow. In the process, he had to abdicate the British throne, surrendered to his brother and accepted to he sent as Governor in Barbados in West Indies. Such things do happen the ways, the 'fancies' can result in! A similar example can be cited to a man 'smitten' by an ugly ill-shaped woman!

Kashmiri Proverb # 30

DAFTAM TE' PAKAI

दफतम तु पकय

دفتم تہ پکئی

Meaning: DAFTAM = Tell me

TE' = And

PAKAI = Shall walk/move.

Tell me and I shall move.

Usage: Reference here is to a person who solicits instruction and guidance from others before taking any action on his part. Obviously he is a person incapable of taking any decision independently, but is nevertheless eager to spare no effort to deliver the goods as per instruction from the guide. Lack of confidence in himself, absence of leadership quality, paucity of original ideas, excessive concern over likely failures and eagerness to remain blame-free can be the reasons for a person to opt for a simple life, more as a page boy than as a helmsman. He is pleased if nothing is lost, even if nothing is gained!

Kashmiri Proverb # 31

DASTAARAN CHHUH NAH MOUL, DARBAARAN CHHUH

दसतारन छु नु मोल, दरबारन छु

دستارن چھو نہ مول،دربارن چھو

Meaning: DASTAARAN* = Turbans

CCHUH = Is

NA = No

MOUL = Price/Worth

DARBAARAN = Professions.

*The turban, especially in Kashmir, would signify the honourable standing and identity of a person in society as well as at workplace.

Turbans may not be worthy, but professions are.

Usage: Merely by wearing a turban, a person may not earn as much respect and recognition as from his status in society or from the excellence shown in the profession he is engaged in.

Well-meaning people accord importance to a man for what he is genuinely worth, and not for his external appearance. And the man's worth is judged from his deeds and character. A turban, however elegant or luxurious it may be, will not conceal the blemishes of a man with dubious character. The society will not accord him any respect.

Kashmiri Proverb # 32

DEESHITH GOESH LAAGUN

डीशिथ गोश लागुन

ڈیشیت گوٚش لاگون

Meaning: DEESHITH = On seeing

GOESH = Silent

LAAGUN = Pretend/Remain.

Feigning innocence/silence on seeing.

Usage: This proverb is about people who observe things and events around them with keen interest and in great detail, yet pretend to be unaware and unconcerned. Such persons are not usually inclined to divulge the information gathered by them to others in their midst. Being sharp in observation and secretive about facts thus gathered may be virtues for those who wish to work in an intelligence system or undercover agency. In the society around us, however, the reluctance to share information with others and inclination to feign ignorance about facts cannot be seen as virtues.

Another saying in Kashmiri having a similar meaning is 'Kalis doel laagun' (कॅलिस डोल लागुन), referring to a person who pretends not to have understood what you said to him. This also applies to a person who shows least interest in sharing any responsibility or contribute to any good cause for the society.

Kashmiri Proverb # 33

DEMINEN KOUNG

डेमिन्यन कौगं

ڈیمینینن کونگ

Meaning: DEMINEN = Sheep's stomach

KOUNG = Saffron.

Sheep's guts with saffron.

Usage: The proverb is about a dish prepared from sheep's viscera comprising stomach, intestines, and offal, all components of what is regarded as inferior meat, but cooked in an exotic style using the choicest, expensive condiments like saffron, to augment its aroma and flavour. It is well known that saffron is a very rare and costly food ingredient used only with high quality meat.

Implicit in the proverb are articles of low quality packaged in decorative caskets to attract buyers' attention and interest, and in the process, lure them into purchasing them. The proverb also seems to sound like a metaphor for people with doubtful merit and values spreading an aroma of distinction by virtue of their polished behaviour and appearance much like the saffron-enriched viscera dish!

Kashmiri Proverb # 34

DHAARI BHAR DHITH BATTE' KHHYUN

दारि बर दिथ बतॖ ख्योन

دھاری بھر دیت بتہ خیون

Meaning: DHAARI = Windows

BHAR = Doors

DHITH = Closed

BATTE' = Rice/Food

KHHYUN = To eat.

Eating food behind closed doors and windows.

Usage: This proverb hints at a family that is singularly aloof, secretive and taciturn, and would not want to share any information even with the closest neighbour. The family could be introvertive and or self-centered. 'Minding own business' may be a virtue up to some level, but remaining isolated from people outside their own family cannot be a welcome trait. In today's world, people have to be outgoing and gregarious because in times of need, next-door friends alone would matter.

Kashmiri Proverb # 35

DIKH NA TAH PAIZAAR KHET

दिख नय तु पुज़ार ख्मतु

دیکھ نہ تہ پیزار خیت

Meaning: DIKH = Give

NA = Not

TAH = If

PAIZAAR = Shoe

KHET = After eating.

Shall give back after eating the shoes.

Usage: Eating shoes is an expression for being beaten with a shoe! The proverb happens to be the routinely adopted dialogue between the victim and the wrong doer, the criminal. The former warns the latter that he/she better do the needful or else shall be forced to do so after getting beaten with shoes (here, meaning to receive a harsh treatment!)

In other words, the proverb means that, 'you shall give-in I know, but only after receiving a harsh treatment!

Also, 'putting on the screws to recover a debt!'

Kashmiri Proverb # 36

DIL BA DIL GAV IANAH, YUT WUCHHAM, TYUT WUCHHAI

दिल ब दिल गव ऑन्, युथ वुछहॉम, तिथुय वुछै

دِل بہ دِل گو عئینہ،یوت وچھم، تیوت وچھُے

Meaning: DIL BA DIL = Your and my heart

GAV = Is

IANAH = Mirror

WUCHHAM = As you see

TYUT = So

WUCHHAI = Shall I see you.

Your heart and mine are like a mirror, as you see me, so shall I appear to you.

Usage: The proverb states that in normal, routine situations, folks react in a manner they are approached, either party observing the protocol; being a business relationship none gets involved emotionally. However, in friendship once intimacy develops this equation changes its colour to become mirror images of each other. Also, it means that, 'so shall I appear, as you see me appear to you!'

Or, 'be friendly and I will be friendly and vice-versa!'

People are lucky, if they can find their views reflected in each other, though such may occur rarely. In case it does, may help resolve disputes amicably between the parties concerned .It is universally true that it takes two hands to clap but one hand to slap! The world order does not function one way!

Kashmiri Proverb # 37

DONH UNGOJAN CHHUH NERAAN TAAS

दोन ऑगुजन छु नेरान टास

دون اونگجن چھو نران ٹاس

Meaning: DONH = Two

UNGOJAN = Fingers

CHHUH = Will

NERAAN = Results

TAAS = Sounds/Snap

It takes two fingers to snap.

Usage: The proverb states that it takes two fingers to act together to snap or make some sort of sound and not with one. Such gestures are resorted to for subtle, friendly or otherwise communication. This may be to invite attention, friendly or otherwise. Consenting friends could drop hints to find solutions to a complicated problem by exploring and expressing one's excitement by snapping of fingers.

There are many more examples with a similar meaning, viz; it takes two hands to clap, two wings to fly, two legs to walk, two people to tango and it takes two hearts to love yours and mine. Not to mention of, it takes two to strike a quarrel!

Kashmiri Proverb # 38

DOUBBE' SUNDH TSHHALUN NENNI EASE DOH

दोेब्य सुन्द छलुन ननि ईज़ दोह

دھوبی سوند چھلون نّی ایز دوہ

Meaning: DOUBBE' = Washerman

SUNDH = Of

TSHHALUN = Washing

NENNI = Will be known

EASE = Eid

DOH = Day.

The washerman's performance (washing quality) will be known on the Eid day.

Usage: The quality of the task accomplished by the doer, say, a craftsman, will be revealed on the 'D-day'. Similarly, the culinary skill of a chef will be known only after the broth is tasted by people just as the quality of work put up by a student will be known only on the day the results are declared. It is equally important to acknowledge that for any given task, people may not be interested to know how it is done as long as the end result is satisfactory.

F

Kashmiri Proverb # 39

FALAK NA PHIKRI KHASAAN

फलख न फिकिरि खसान

فلک نہ فکری خصان

Meaning: FALAK = Sky

NA = No

PHIKRI-KHASAAN = Give damn.

(An arrogant person doesn't) Give a damn even to sky/ zenith.

Usage: This one is about a conceited person who does not care two hoots for anyone, no matter how high and mighty the latter may be. This person is so intoxicated with the success he has attained in securing position, wealth or even knowledge, and thus believes he has reached the ultimate in life. The success apparently has gone into his head, prompting an arrogant bchaviour.

G

Kashmiri Proverb # 40

GA'NZ NASS

गन्ज़ नस

گنز نص

Meaning: GANZ = Insensitive/Blind

NASS = Nose.

A blind nose.

Usage: A person with 'Ganz Nass' does not notice or smell anything unusual in an atmosphere swamped by stench. After being exposed to an intensely fetid ambience for a long time, even a normal man can get so desensitized that he may find the odour no more disagreeable, or may not even perceive its prevalence. His smell buds would be dead or disabled by prolonged exposure to the unpleasant atmosphere. It is a well-known fact that people who live near garbage dumps and stenchy drains do get immune to the foul air.

The scope of loss of olfactory sensitivity can be broadened to include similar losses in other human faculties too. Bureaucrats and politicians entering into an already – weakened and non-functioning system of governance may lose their sensitivity to issues faced by the general public. They are most likely to develop 'Ganz Nass'.

Note: There is a locality in Srinagar called 'Ganz Khud'. Here, the tanners process leather which gives out a pungent and foul smell. People living and working there do not, however, feel the stench as they have developed insensitiveness to it. There is an interesting story about 'Ganz Khud'.

Kashmiri Proverb # 41

GAA'NTI THOOL VAALUN

गाँन्टि ठूल वालुन

گانٹ ٹھول والون

Meaning: GAAN'TI = Eagle*

THOOL = Egg

VAALUN = Bringing down

*Common Pariah Kite.

Bringing down the eagle's egg from her nest.

Usage: The nest of an eagle is usually built at the top-most branch of a tree where the mother bird lays her eggs. It is almost impossible for anyone to gather these eggs and bring them down safely to the ground. The task is rendered harder because of the watchful, hawkish eyes of the mother guarding the eggs and the nest.

Encountering hard and impossible tasks is part of a man's daily life. Situations of this kind are portrayed in other proverbs too, in every language. 'BONI MUHUL TAARUN' is one in Kashmiri that relates to attempting to pierce a chinar tree with a wooden pestle which is just impossible. This proverb is also used to describe a situation in which it becomes difficult to win an argument, take a decision or when caught in a dilemma/catch-22 situation when we say, the job is like: 'GAANTI' THOOL VAALUN'.

Kashmiri Proverb # 42

GAAWIH CHHUH WOUNAMUT HATTIH KINI DITAM TAH LATTIH KINI DIMAI

गावि छु वोनमुत हटि किन्य दितम, तु लटि किन्य दिमय

گاویہ چھو ونموت ہٹھی کینی دیتم تہ لٹھی کینی دمئی

Meaning: GAAWIH = Cow

CHHUH = Has

WOUNAMUT = Said

HATTIH = Throat

KINI = Through

DITAM = Give

TAH = And

LATTIH = Tail

DIMAI = Shall give.

The cow says, 'Give to me through throat and I shall give you through tail.'

Usage: This proverb upholds the spirit of 'give and take' latent in a cow's promise to the master that if he takes care of her with adequate quantities of nourishing food, she would reciprocate with a copious supply of milk.

There is an old saying that if you satiate your servant or a pet animal with delectable food, you can expect sincere service. It is as if relationships are all governed by the concept of reciprocity. Such a conditional link also exists between an employer and employees in any organization. It also plays a role in the relationship among members of the society and, in a latent form, even within a family.

For the successful management of a family or an enterprise, such a spirit of 'give and take' and a philosophy of 'forgive and forget' are prerequisites.

Kashmiri Proverb # 43

GABIH BUTHIH RAMAH-HUN

गॊबि बुथि राम्-हून

گبہ ہوتھی رامہ-ہون

Meaning: GABIH = Sheep's

BUTHIH = Face of

RAMAH-HOON = Wolf.

A sheep by face, but wolf in real.

Usage: This phrase is a jocular variant of the metaphor 'a wolf in sheep's clothing,' symbolizing a person who appears friendly and harmless but is deeply hostile, indeed someone who hides malicious intent under the guise of looking benevolent. One is reminded of the saying 'do not be carried away by the words of the salesmen at the store; they are all wolves in sheep's clothing.' Jesus is said to have exhorted his followers to 'beware of false prophets that come in sheep's clothing, but inwardly they are ravening wolves.' From appearance alone it is hard to identify deceitful and crafty persons. One has to be cautious and circumspect while dealing with such people.

Kashmiri Proverb # 44

GAEIR GOJIH*

गॉरय़ गोजि

گیٔر گوجھ

Meaning: GAEIR = Water-chestnut (Singharah)

GOJIH = Kernel.

*Come Spring and one can see, all over Kashmir, raw water-chestnut (Gaeir) being roasted and decorticated to extract the kernel (Gojih) which is eaten, generally with a pinch of salt. No expertise or intelligence is needed for this task. The words 'gaeir gojih' are used to describe those who don't use their brain.

The kernel of water-chestnut.

Usage: Kashmiris use this proverb as an abusive or derogatory phrase while describing or addressing a dull, dim-witted person. The phrase is also used in the context of a simpleton who cannot appreciate or understand things with conventional speed, or make correct judgement of events happening around him. The person with such poor capability, often viewed as a duffer, faces deprecatory rebuke such as 'Oh, you gaier gojih! Why don't you try to understand what is happening?', which is an equivalent of calling a person, 'You numbskull!'

Kashmiri Proverb # 45

GAGUR CHHUH KARAAN BRARIS MAAT

गगुर छु करान ब्रॉरिस मात

گھگور چھو کران برریس مات

Meaning: GAGUR = Rat

CHHUH = Is

KARAAN = Does

BRARIS = Cat

MAAT = Outsmarts.

The rat outsmarts the cat.

Usage: The rat, being much more agile and smaller in size compared to the cat, can easily outrun and dodge its sworn enemy, and eventually escape unhurt. The rat can thus emerge as the winner in the deadly chase despite its inherent weaknesses.

In the lives of human beings too, one comes across situations in which a humble and seemingly weak individual defeats a mighty one by virtue of hidden strengths about which his adversary may be unaware of.

It will be too presumptuous to expect that the big and mighty shall always win the game.

Kashmiri Proverb # 46

GARAH GAV CHHAKAH-NAAV,
DAKAH DAKAH PAKNAAV

घरु गव चक्कु-नाव,
दकु दकु पकुनाव

گرہ گوو چھٔکہ-ناو،دکہ دکہ پکناؤ

Meaning: GARAH = Home/House

GAV = Is

CHHAKAH-NAV* = Barge/Large boat

DAKAH = Pushing

PAKNAAV = Move.

Home is like a huge barge that demands enormous effort to propel forward.

*Chhakah-Naav is a massive barge usually loaded with weeds, and silt gathered from the depths of Dal lake or its backwaters, both cargoes possessing quality as rich manure. Sometimes, the barge is laden with stumps of forest trees called as 'HAQ' (हक) or (حق), used in winter as fire wood. The barges are usually loaded almost to the brim, leaving only an inch or so to ensure safety. They are towed to the destination and unloaded.

Usage: Here Chhakah-Nav is compared with a home wherein the head of the family has to perform acrobatics of not only balancing the heavily laden boat but also propelling it forward. The home may consist of people of all ages and temperaments, likes and dislikes. Managing all of them single handedly demands utmost care and presence of mind on the part of the head of the family because it is his responsibility to take everyone along. A little oversight on his part can spell disaster for all. Running day-to-day affairs in the family is indeed a tight-rope walk for him much like maneuvering the overloaded barge.

Kashmiri Proverb # 47

GARIBAS GOBUR ZAAV, ONUN KATI?

गॅरीबस गोबर ज़ाव, ओनुन कति?

غرییس گوبور زاؤ،اونون کتی

Meaning: GARIBAS = Poor man

GOBUR = Son

ZAAV = Born

ONUN = Brought

KATI = From where.

Wherefrom a poor man brought the new born son?

Usage: In a society/group of people, over time, get accustomed to each other's presence and treat each other casually building a normal and even society. Eyebrows get raised once any unusual, out-of-the-box, happening takes place that attracts the attention of others. This could occur, say once a humble person is bestowed with an unusually beautiful baby, someone begets a huge lottery/success in profession/business, etc. Or, someone's child succeeds in a highly competitive examination thereby, making him/her self-eligible for a pretty lucrative job etc. All such unusual happenings cause folks to look askance, jealousy being inherent such ones from the butt of gossip. Others wonder how someone among them achieved success?

It is human nature that happiness is not relished and a pauper's prosperity puzzles all!

Kashmiri Proverb # 48

GARRI-PYATT ZAAMTUR GAV BHAR-TALUK HOON

गॅरिप्यठ ज़ामतुर गव बरतलुक हून

گری پیٹھ زامتور گوو بھرتعلق ہون

Meaning: GARRI-PYATT = Live-in

ZAAMTUR = Son-in-law

GAV = Is/Shall be

BHAR-TALUK = At the entrance door

HOON = Dog.

A son-in-law who lives in his wife's home* will assume the status of a dog standing at the entrance (waiting to pick up morsels).

*Such an event is viewed with contempt in Indian (Hindu) culture.

Usage: A person living in another's house as a permanent guest tends to lose his pre-eminence and gets gradually relegated to an inferior status.

In the native context, the son-in-law of a family usually maintains a subtle emotional distance from his spouse's kins whereby his respectability stays aloft. This distance, however, gets obliterated in case of a live-in son-in-law! The irrefutable natural law: 'familiarity breeds contempt' begins to operate. It is tough indeed to maintain a balance between closeness of relationships and the emotional distance.

Kashmiri Proverb # 49

GOOER VOVHO TSHAA WOTSH MARAAN

गूर्य वोहवोह छा वॊछ् मरान

گور وہ-وہ چّھہا وہچّھ مران

Meaning: GOOER = Milkman (who supplies milk)

VOVOH = Curse/Swear

TSHAA = Is

WOTSH = Calf

MARAAN = Dies.

Milk-man's curses showered upon a calf, that shares the milk yield of the mother do not harm the calf.

Usage: Curses and invectives hurled by a milkman on a calf sharing milk cause no harm/death to the latter. Equally harmless are angry words from seniors in the family, society or workplaces, uttered perhaps at moments of frustration, only to be treated as reprimand for future corrections.

Thus, one should not get unnecessarily provoked or hassled or feel bad about it.

Kashmiri Proverb # 50

GUDANUK SAUDA GATSHIH NAH RAWARUN

ग्वडन्युक सोदा गछि नु रावुरुन

گڑنوک سودا گچِینی راؤرون

Meaning: GUDANUK = First

SAUDA = Deal/Offer

GATSHIH NAH = Never refuse

RAWARUN = Lose.

One (a businessman) must not let go the first offer.

Usage: This is an advice for a shopkeeper or a vender, translated verbatim mean, 'do not lose your first customer'! This advice is purely sentimental and may have no scientific basis/reason. In our effort to start off a day with a smile, a positive note/approach is desirable and encouraging environment is most welcome.

Kashmiri traders, like those of other places and even some European countries, are very superstitious about refusing the offer of the day's first customer. To that effect, they will frequently rather lose a little in the profit margin than allow the buyer to depart without purchasing!

Kashmiri Proverb # 51

GUR GARIH TAH NAKHAASAS MUAL PRICCHAAN

गूर गरि तु नख़ासस मोल प्रछान

گور گریھ تہ نخاسس مول پریچّھان

Meaning: GUR = Horse

GARIH = At home

TAH = And

NAKHAASAS* = Designated Officer for the sale of animals (here, horses)

MUAL = Price

PRICCHAAN = Asking.

*Nakhaas (नख़ास) is an officially designated place (Bazaar) for trading of animals. 'Nakhaasas', is a designated officer for fixing the price of animals.

Keeping horse at home and inquire its price from the designated officer.

Usage: The character in this proverb is the owner of a horse desirous of selling the animal for which he stops by a 'Nakhaas' so as to assess the prevailing rates without actually taking the 'merchandise' with him. Either the person is not serious about selling the horse or wishes to merely watch the market trend. It is also likely that he is just passing time and, in the process, making a fool of himself. He must understand that one can sell the goods only by physically presenting them to the prospective buyers, in accordance with normal trade practice, whatever may be the type of merchandise.

Similar is the situation when a person goes to a boy's home with a marriage proposal for his daughter without taking her along, but hoping that the party would agree to the proposal despite the girl's absence. Serious things cannot be accomplished in such a simplistic manner. Both parties in a deal have the prerogative, and the need, to assess the worth of what is intended to be transacted.

Kashmiri Proverb # 52

GUR, ZANANAH TAH SHAMSHER, YIM TRENAWAI CHHIH BE-WAFAA

गुर, ज़नान् तु शमशेर, यिम त्रेनवय छि बेवफ़ा

گور،زنانہ تہ شمشیر،ییم ترینوای چھیہ بیوفا

Meaning: GUR = Horse

ZANANAH = Woman

TAH = And

SHAMSHER = Sword

YIM = These

TRENAWAI = All three

CHHIH = Are

BE-WAFAA = Unfaithful.

A horse, a woman (wife) and a sword; these three are untrustworthy.

Usage: This proverb has been coined based upon real life experiences of our elders/ancestors in their day-to-day activities.

A woman could be a turncoat, have let out state secrets for pelf, jewellery, state power, etc., attempted to take side. While a sword is a double edged weapon which could be used as desired being an inanimate object. However, a horse is less known as an unfaithful towards its owner.

Nevertheless, all the three can deceive you, when they are expected to be faithful.

There is a Persian saying similar in meaning, 'asb[1] o zan[2] o shamsher wafadaar na baashad'*

'اسب، زن،شمشیر وفادار نہ باشد'

[1]Asb = Horse

[2]Zan = Woman.

Kashmiri Proverb # 53

GURIN LAGIK NAAL TAH KHAR GAI (AAYI) PADAR DARIT (HYATH)

गुर्यन लॉगिख नाल तु खर आयि पडर दॉरिथ

گورین لگیک نال تہ خر گئی(آئی) پڑر دریت (ہتھ)

Meaning: GURIN = Horses

LAGIK = Put on

NAAL = Shoes

TAH = And

KHAR = Donkeys

GAI = Went

AAYI = Came

PADAR = Hoofs

DARIT = Forwarded

HYATH = With.

The horses put on their horseshoes and the donkeys came forward for nailing their hooves.

Usage: Customarily, it is the horses that get shoes fixed with nails on their hooves but, the proverb says, in a veiled sarcasm, donkeys too come forward to get shoes fixed on their hooves. What is implied here is the eagerness of an inferior guy to occupy a place at par with the elite. The situation smacks of a virtual competition between them unequal.

It is implied in the proverb that every man is ordained to occupy a certain position in society and perform functions as demanded by his rank. It is also hinted that one should not seek or desire what is beyond one's position and entitlement.

There are examples in Hindu scriptures where status mismatch hampered performance. In the epic Mahabharata, Karna, the best archer of that time was not allowed to compete in a royal skill contest merely because he was not a prince. Similarly, Abhimanyu was not allowed to qualify as an archer for fear that he could in that event supersede a prince and create imbalance in the order of royalty.

Kashmiri Proverb # 54

GYAV KHEWAAN TAH GARDANIH KUN ATTAH LAAGAAN

ग्यव ख्यवान तु गरदनि कुन अथु लागान

گیو خیوان تہ گردانہ کون اتھ لاگان

Meaning: GYAV = Ghee

KHEWAAN = Eating

TAH = And

GARDANIH KUN = Towards Neck

ATTAH = Hand

LAAGAAN = Touches.

Eating ghee and touching the neck with hand.

Usage: There is a common belief that the neck fattens by eating ghee. Even as he is swallowing clumps of this delicacy, a person keeps checking with his palm and fingers to ascertain whether his neck has already started getting fat!

The allusion here is to a simpleton who is expecting instant result for his actions. He does not possess the patience to let things take their own natural course towards the expected outcome. While scoffing at the fretful ghee gobbler, the proverb seems to applaud the value of perseverance and composure while grappling with problems in our daily lives. Patience indeed pays!

Kashmiri Proverb # 55

HAALAV MARAN MAGAR DAANESS DITH DAAH

हालव मरन, मगर दानस दिथ दाह

حالاؤ مرن مگر،دانیس دیت داہ

Meaning: HAALAV = Locusts

MARAN = Die

MAGAR = But

DAANES = Paddy crop

DITH = After

DAAH* = Destroyed/Consumed.

*DAAH, is a term used for performing the last rites before cremation of a dead body.

Locusts will die but, only after destroying the paddy crop.

Usage: During summer season, swarms of locusts breed in the deserts of Arabia and travel in huge cloud-like formations, into the Indian subcontinent. The invasion of the farms occurs when the crops of paddy and wheat are in full bloom. Humidity and warm temperatures encourage their local breeding and further multiplication.

At sunset the locusts settle on the crop and, in one night, gobble up the whole crop. By daybreak the insects, in humongous numbers, resume their onward journey. Within a few weeks, their life cycle comes to an end.

The proverb sums up the locust story, implying that certain events, albeit their brief duration, cause lasting devastation much like the now-familiar 'tsunami'. It would always be advisable to take some preventive measures to lessen the damage likely to occur, though impossible to completely control it.

Kashmiri Proverb # 56

HAAPTH YAARAZ

हापथ यारज़

حاپتھ یارض

Meaning: HAAPUT = Wild bear

YAARAZ = Friendship.

Friendship with a bear.

Usage: The proverb is extracted from the story of a man who befriended a wild bear while working in a forest. Over time, the friendship grew strong and the bear started bringing honey for his friend to eat. One day while relishing the honey, the man fell asleep, with the sweet liquid smeared over his lips and cheeks, attracting bees. In a bid to save the friend from the sting of bees, the bear picked up a heavy stone and slammed it on the man's face. The stone frightened away the bees but killed the man. Although the intention of the bear was noble, the outcome was disastrous. The friendship outreach boomeranged on the man.

The proverb is an affirmation of the futility and dangers of friendship with rash and foolish people who, despite their good intent, might bring more harm than good. It also carries the message that people must be discreet and circumspect while selecting friends.

Kashmiri Proverb # 57

HAKIMAS TAH HAAKIMAS NISHI RACHHTAM KHUDAAYO

हकीमस तु हॉकिमस निशि रछुम ख्वदायो

حکیمس تہ حاکمس نشي رچھتم خدایو

OR

HUKUM-I-HAAKIM O HAKIM CHHUH MARG-I-MUFAAJAAT

हुक्म-इ-हाकिम ओ हकीम छु मरग-इ-मुफ़ाजात

حوکم- ای- حاکمِ او حکیم چھو مرگ- ای- مفاجات

Meaning: HAKIMAS = Doctor

TAH = And

HAAKIMAS = Ruler

NISHI = From

RACHHTAM = Keep away

KHUDAAYO = O God

HUKUM = Order

MARG = Death

MUFAAJAAT* = Unexpected/Untimely.

*Arabic, مفاجات, मुफ़ाजात।

O God, keep me away from the doctor and the ruler.

Or

The ruler's and the doctor's orders are like sudden death.

Usage: The proverb cautions/advises the people to maintain a safe distance between themselves and the medical doctor and similarly for the ruler/sovereign, their ilk. For doing so, one cannot, under normal circumstances, challenge the decisions pronounced by either. To challenge either's authority would amount to disturbing a hornet's nest.

Also, their orders must be obeyed quickly lest, one should face their wrath, which may result in a harsh punishment.

Kashmiri Proverb # 58

HALAALAS HISAAB TAH HARAAMAS AZAAB

हलालस हिसाब तु हरामस अज़ाब

حلالس حساب تہ حرامس عذاب

Meaning: HALAALAS = Legal/permissible

HISAAB = Here, means Rewarded

HARAAMAS = Illegal

AZAAB = Punishment/difficulty.

Lawful means fetch rewards; unlawful, hardships.

Usage: There is an old saying, 'Honesty is the best policy', which holds true universally and for all the times. Legal and honest earnings, however small, bestow satisfaction and mental peace besides perhaps bringing further fortune.

In contrast, ill-gotten wealth is bound to remain a source of discomfort, and shall keep its recipient on tenterhooks all the time, with the fear of the long arms of law catching up with him, sooner or later. Life indeed will remain miserable for him.

Honesty is a major component of what is referred to as moral character which also encompasses attributes like kindness, discipline, and integrity, all of which are important in one's life.

Kashmiri Proverb # 59

HALI TI SHRAAKH, BALI TI SHRAAKH

हलि ति श्राख, बलि ति श्राख

حلی تی شراق،بلی تی شراق

Meaning: HALI = Front side of human body between ribcage & hip-bone, near navel

TI = Is

SHRAAKH = Sword

BALI = Rear part of human body; opposite of Hali.

Sword is pointing both from the front and the rear of the body.

Usage: When a situation arises compelling a person to make a choice between a deep well on one side and a cavernous gorge on the other, we use this proverb which literally means that there is a sword hanging in front of the body and another behind this person in distress. Either way he is destined to face a catastrophe. 'Between the devil and the deep sea' is an equivalent English proverb that describes the dilemma of a sailor faced with two equally awful choices of undertaking repair of the ship risking his life, or leaving the entire ship at risk by not repairing it. It is thus a Hobson's choice for this person who confronts the necessity of accepting one of the two equally unpleasant alternatives.

Kashmiri Proverb # 60

HARI TAH TOTAS VANUN

हारि तु तोतस वनुन

ہری تہ توتس ونون

Meaning: HARI = Sparrow

TAH = And

TOTAS = Parrot

VANUN = To say and speak

To speak to sparrow and parrot.

Usage: The proverb when translated verbatim reads, 'to speak to a bird, sparrow and a parrot', who wouldn't understand what you are talking about?

This proverb is used when any advice/suggestion given by an experienced/senior person in the society/family or even workplace and is considered as casual/insignificant, unimportant and even dinky by the takers, we call that equivalent to talking to sparrow and parrots.

Also, when an elderly parent trying to speak words of wisdom to the siblings, who do not appreciate and find the jargon boring almost calling it as falling on deaf ears. Talking thus, becomes inconsequential, futile and waste of time!

Kashmiri Proverb # 61

HARKAT KAR TAH BARKAT KARI

हरकथ कर तु बरकथ करी

حرکت کر تہ برکت کری

Meaning: HARKAT KAR = Do some activity

TAH = And

BARKAT = Blessed

KARI = Be.

Indulge in activities and stay blessed.

Usage: This proverb conveys the message that effort made on a good cause will always be rewarded with dividends. It seems to exhort people to keep working not only to achieve success but also to earn goodwill from God. English and Persian versions of the proverb read: 'God/Heaven helps those who help themselves '(Himmata-e-Marda, Madada-e-Khuda) (हिम्मते-ए-र्मदां, मददे-ए-ख़ुदां) (ہمت مردا،مدد خدا)'

The merit of self-reliance is illustrated in Aesop's fable in which Hercules the God of power advises the Cartman caught in a mire to use his will and skill to help himself instead of merely seeking divine intervention. Self-reliance comes naturally to people who abhor idling, and uphold the maxim 'work is worship'. Such persons will certainly be rewarded.

Kashmiri Proverb # 62

HATTIS KHASH TAH HAUNGANI MITHI

हॉटिस खश तु हॉंगुनि मीठ्य

ہٹس خش تہ ہنگنی میٹھ

Meaning: HATIS = Throat

KHASH = Axe/cut

TAH = And/But

HANGANI = Chin

MITHI = Kisses.

Kisses on the chin but axe on the throat.

Usage: The proverb states that where your (feigned) friend would be kissing your chin/lower lip and simultaneously with his other hand placing a knife on your neck in an effort to kill you. Such situation is defined by this proverb.

This action would be tantamount to killing through deceit. There have occurred many such killings committed by traitors in history where, for occupying the throne/state power, even brothers have resorted to such killings through deceit.

Aurangzeb killed his own elder brother Darasheeko after inviting him for a drink and chained him with silver handcuffs and occupied the throne, leaving him to die!

Kashmiri Proverb # 63

HISAAB GAV BABAS TE GOBRAS

हिसाब गव् बबस तु गॊबुरस

حساب گاؤ ببس تہ گوبرس

Meaning: HISAAB = Clear transaction

GAV = Is/should be

BABAS = Father

TE = And/between

GOBRAS = Son.

Transactions should be transparent between father and son.

Usage: The proverb advises that to maintain any and every relationship in a healthy mode, there has got to be a mutual give and take understanding. This applies even to the relationship between a father and his son or the offspring or between close friends. This is an essential requirement especially, in business and money matters. No lopsided relationship/transaction can remain stable/healthy, if parties tend to be selfish. Mutual give and take is the essence for any sustainable relationship. Experience has shown, time and again, that many families/close friendships get ruined because of the mistrust brewing up due to not keeping their clear and clean accounts between themselves. Thus, reciprocity is an important corner stone for maintaining a healthy relationship!

Kashmiri Proverb # 64

HOOEN LOET SYUED KARUN

हून्य लोट स्योद करुन

ہوٴئین لوٹھ سیید کرون

Meaning: HOOEN = Dog's

LOET = Tail

SYUED = Straighten

KARUN = To

To straighten a dog's tail.

Usage: This proverb literally means that a dog's tail can never be straightened, even if this appendage is drawn into a pipe and left there for years. The tail would bend back to its crooked state as soon as it is released from the pipe. The effort made in this unproductive endeavour is as wasteful as trying to whiten charcoal with cosmetic creams and lotions! Many worldly things, living and non-living, do not change because they seem destined to remain stagnant in appearance and behaviour though the world as a whole is ever-changing and dynamic.

The proverb gains relevance in life situations which are quite common. One such situation relates to people's mindset refusing change despite pressure from all around. In different walks of life we come across people with rigid views and idiosyncrasies that cannot be altered or influenced by external forces. Mending their ways is as hard as straightening a dog's tail.

Kashmiri Proverb # 65

HOON VORAAN TE' KAARKHAAN CHALAAN

हून वोरान तु कारखानु चलान

'ہون ووران تہ کارخان چلان

Meaning: HOON = Dog

VORAAN = Barks

TE' = And

KAARKHAAN = Factory

CHALAAN = Working.

Factory will continue working, despite barking dogs.

Usage: Work in a factory will go on unhampered despite barking of dogs in the vicinity. What the proverb implies is that a robust institution will keep functioning smoothly even if hurdles are placed by disloyal workers. Similarly at personal level, a man/woman with courage will not be cowed down by impediments placed by his/her adversaries.

The proverb also echoes an Arabic/Persian saying: 'the dogs bark but the caravan goes on' (हून वोरान तु कारवां पकान'), which is meant to convey that if your intention is good and effort is made in the right direction, negative forces can be ignored and you can move along. The dog may as well bark at the moon.

Kashmiri Proverb # 66

HOUN ASIN MAGAR KUNS MAH ASIN

हून ऑसिन मगर कूंस मु ऑसिन

ہون اسین مگر کونس مہ اسین

Meaning: HOUN = Dog

ASIN = Be

MAGAR = But

KUNS = Youngest son

MAH = Not.

Better to be a dog, but not the youngest son.

Usage: In our South Asia society, the youngest child (here, son) happens to be fondled by all the seniors, hence they sort of assume having their right over him. This results in him getting used as an errand boy or say everyone's handy man to get any sundry jobs done. In a way, the youngest is patronised by the rest, hence feels exploited. At times, he feels miserable as to why he is being used and exploited by virtue of him being the youngest and feels that the dogs are perhaps better off than him.

As they say, the youngest are generally the father's butt, the mother's scorn and the brother's fag. There is a similar Persian proverb, stating:

'Sag[1] bash khurd[2] ma bash'

(सग[1] बाश खुर्द[2] मा बाश)

(سگ۱ باش خورد۲ مہ باش)

meaning, it is better to be dog but not the younger son.

[1]Dog

[2]Small (here, youngest)

I

Kashmiri Proverb # 67

ILLAT GALIH TAH AAADAT GALIH NAH

इल्लत गलि तु आदथ गलि न्

علت گلی تہ عادت گلی نہ

Meaning: ILLAT = Sickness

GALIH = Will go

TAH = But

AADAT = Habit

NAH = No

The sickness may go, but the habit will not.

Usage: This Kashmiri proverb illustrates the well-known truth that health disorders of man can be diagnosed and remedied whereas habits and idiosyncrasies, particularly those nurtured over many years are hard to abandon. It was Benjamin Franklin who in 1780 had remarked: 'old habits die hard'. In course time, these sane words have attained status as a proverb in many languages.

The habits can include both desirable as well as despicable kinds. Helping nature, polite manners, humility, empathy and other desirable traits will forever remain with some people even if they pass through mentally stressful times. Even more enduring are unwholesome and obnoxious habits like addiction to alcohol and narcotics, penchant to use of foul language, kleptomania, dishonesty, etc., acquired over a period of time. There is no known cure for such proclivities.

Kashmiri Proverb # 68

INSAAN CHHUH POSHIH KHUTAH AAWULL TAH KANIH KHUTAH DUR

इन्सान छु पोशि खॊतु ऑव्युल तु कनि खॊतु दॊर

انسان چھو پوشیہ خوتہ اوئل تہ کنیہ خوتہ دور

Meaning: INSAAN = Man/Person

CHHUH = Is

POSHIH = Flower

KHUTAH = More

AWLL = Weak/Fragile

TAH = And

KANIH = Stone

DUR = Hard.

Human being is more delicate than a flower and yet harder than stone.

Usage: A human being (applicable equally to animals too) can be fragile/sensitive than a flower but time/situation demanding could act tougher than thunder. Upon, both the species, God has bestowed the sense for self-survival/preservation and physically too, both can act pretty tough.

A human being happens to be sensitive physically, also emotionally extremely sensitive to the surrounding environment!

In the case of flowers, 'touch me not', could be an illustration. In the course of a discussion, one could dislodge an opponent by treading on his/her corns!

In some cases, a man's own pain or trouble affects him, but not the tears and pain of another!

Politeness is essential to a human as fragrance to a flower. Rightly said by Sir Fulke Greville, 'As charity covers a multitude of sins before God, so does politeness before men!'

J

Kashmiri Proverb # 69

JAAN CHHUH, PANNUN PAAN

जान छु, पनुन पान

جان چھوه ، پنّون پان

Meaning:

JAAN = Good

CHHUH = Is

PANNUN = My

PAAN = Self.

I only am good.

Usage: There is a another proverb with a similar meaning,' Jaan Kus Chhuh? Pannun Paan'!

Self-aggrandizement is a normal behaviour of any person trying to prove his/her own superiority. He/she attempts to establish, being an inherent part of ego, to retain one's own self-esteem, which is an essential part of self-respecting existence, hence normal.

Good is one's own self and one who is good, will find every one good!

Kashmiri Proverb # 70

**JAWAANAS NAH ROZGAAR; LOKUTIS MAEJ MARINI; TAH
BUDIS AASHIN MARINI.
YIM TRENAWAI KATHAH CHHEH SAKHT MUSIBAT**

जवानस नु रोज़गार; लोकुटिस मॉज मरिन्य; तु बुडस आशेन मरिन्य!
यिमु त्रेनुवय कथु छे सखुत मुसीबथ

جوانس نہ روزگار،لوکٹس میج مران،تہ بوڈیس آشین مرین
ایم ترینوی کتھ چھ سخت مصیبتھ

Meaning: JAWAANAS = Young

NAH = No

ROZGAAR = Job

LUKUTIS = Baby/Child

MAEJ = Mother

MARINI = Dying

TAH = And

BUDIS = Old man

AASHIN = Wife

YIM = These

TRENAWAI = All three

KATHA = Happenings

CHHEH = Are

SAKHT = Terrible

MUSIBAT = Misfortunes.

A young man without job; a mother dying and leaving a baby behind; the wife of an old man dying! These three are terrible misfortunes.

Usage: A youth/young man (woman) without occupation/employment; a child/baby losing his/her mother and an old man becoming a widower, all the three situations happen to be cases of catastrophe. None may/should undergo such a situation! These cases deserve sympathy from the society, family, friends, etc.

Sooner or later, the young man should find a job, shall not stay a devil's workshop for too long, is natural. For the person, losing his spouse, our own strong traditional and family values should prevail in lessening his misery.

The worst victim happens to be the motherless child who would never overcome the deficiency of her unless extremely lucky providence helps him/her.

Kashmiri Proverb # 71

KAAHAN GARAN KUNI TAEV, HIMMAT RAV TAH WANAV KAS?

काहन गरन कुन्यी तॉव, हेम्मथ रॉव तु वनव कस

کاہن گرن کونی طو،ہمت راو تہ ونو کس

Meaning:

KAAHAN = Eleven

GARAN = Houses

KUNI = Only one

TAEV = Pan

HIMMAT = Courage

RAV = Gone/lost

WANAV = Ask

KAS = To whom.

Only one pan for eleven houses; courage lost and whom to ask?

Usage: The proverb states that there is only one frying-pan among eleven households, showing acute scarcity. Such a situation could be the result of poor economic conditions of the concerned families, causing acrimony giving rise to frequent quarrels and blame games. This may lead to great disorder and distress at times among the families. The situation could be remedied through improved earnings and economic management.

Besides, sharing of an item with others usually lead to losing courage to fix responsibility/accountability on anyone, in case any wrong thing happening. Under such conditions, whom one can complain to? When people share resources and if it is damaged, no one would have the courage to blame anyone as it would be difficult to prove.

Kashmiri Proverb # 72

KAAHAN POUTREN HENZ MAIJ VATI PYAT

काहन पोत्रन हुन्ज़ मॉज वति प्यठ

کاہن پوترن ہنز میج وتی پیٹھ

Meaning: KAAHAN = Eleven

POUTREN = Children/Sons

HENZ = Of

MAIJ = Mother

VATI = Road

PYAT = On.

Mother of eleven sons on the road.

Usage: This proverb illustrates an irony of life in which a mother of several children is driven to fend for herself in her old age. This fate often befalls a father too. Shirking his/her moral responsibility, each of the siblings tends to believe that the others are financially and otherwise better equipped to look after the parents and ensure their welfare. Begetting many children was seen in the past as a guarantee for happiness in the twilight years of parents. However, reality often belies expectations. Bereft of filial affection and ethical values, each of the children would try to push the parents on another's shoulders. One cannot help invoking Shakespeare's words of wisdom: 'Fathers that wear rags do make their children blind.'

Kashmiri Proverb # 73

KAM KHYUN, GAM NAH HYUN

कम ख्योन, ग़म नु ह्योन

کم خیون ، گم نہ ہون

Meaning: KAM = Less/little

KHYUN = Eat

GAM = Worry/sorrow

NAH = Not

HYUN = Take.

Better to eat less than bear the grief.

Usage: The proverb advises/suggests a person to be satisfied with whatever meager, he/she may earn and live off a life of satisfaction rather than chasing higher goals entailing tensions. That may otherwise disturb his peace of mind impacting his/her overall well-being!

There is no end to wants/greed! But, one needs to be contented in life rather than to be in the rat race to get more and more at the cost of one's health and peace of mind. There is a proverb/saying in Urdu/Persian with a similar meaning, 'desires lead one to fall in the well/ditch!'

('चाह ही चा मैं गिराती है') ('چاہ ہی چھ میں گراتی ہے')

Here, former 'chah' is desire & latter is a well/ditch!

There is also another Kashmiri proverb, P # 74 ('Kamas Chhuh Kamaal Tah Tsaris Chhuh Zawaal' 'कमस छु कमाल तु च्रिस छु ज़वाल') in this book, which conveys somewhat similar message.

Kashmiri Proverb # 74

KAMAS CHHUH KAMAAL TAH TSARIS CHHUH ZAWAAL

कमस छु कमाल तु च़रिस छु ज़वाल

کمس چھو کمال تہ چریس چھو زوال

Meaning: KAMAS = Less

CHHUH = Is having

KAMAAL = Accomplishment

TAH = And

TSARIS = More/Abundance

ZAWAAL = Decline/Wane.

Less begets accomplishment and abundance, decline.

Usage: This proverb intends to uphold the merits of moderation and the defeat of excesses, and is principally applicable to speaking words and spending money. Expressing ideas in a limited number of words, that too to the point, will be a more effective way of communicating with people than engaging in verbosity. It is indeed wisely said: 'brevity is the soul of wit'. The proverb assumes relevance also in the context of spending money where moderation is equally needed. Extravagance is likely to result in penury if the resources are meagre. The proverb also hints that poverty has the power to unite a family whereas abundance, both of resources and of the style of spending, can cause fissures leading to break-up of a family.

The above prospect may await nations too! If resources are scant, challenges arise. Innovative ways to build resources would be found which otherwise would not have been attempted. It is as if to possess less is blessing in disguise.

Kashmiri Proverb # 75

KANAS BATI LADUN

कनस बतुॱ लदुन

كنس بة لدن

Meaning: KANAS = Ear

BATI* = Cooked rice

LADUN = To fill.

*Here, it means food.

To fill the ear with rice.

Usage: The proverb translated verbatim, the person wishes to convey emphatically that he/she surely puts the food in the mouth rather than in the 'ear'. The person is pretty experienced, knowledgeable, clever/smart and matured enough who cannot be fooled around/way laid and has not wasted his/her years!

The person tries to convey others not to be under the impression that he cannot look through their machinations and thus, says 'I do not put my food into my ear'!

More often the use of such a statement is resorted to while discussing on some important issues or hammering out a commercial negotiation where chances of waylaying/ deceiving by the counterpart, i.e., the adversary happens to be greater.

Kashmiri Proverb # 76

KANDAS TAH MUJIH KUNUI SAAD

कन्दस तु मुजि कुनुय साद

کندس تہ موجھ کنوئی ساد

Meaning: KANDAS = Sugar-candy

TAH = And

MUJIH = Radish

KUNUI = Same

SAD = Taste.

Candy and radish have same taste.

Usage: The proverb explains the comparison between the two opposite/extremes, a sugar-candy, naturally tastes sweet and soothing in the mouth whereas, a good and worthy of its name, the radish causes a strange pungent burning sensation of the mouth, though enjoyable in its own manner or style yet may cause to well-up tears! These are the two extremes and defy comparison!

Similarly, sometimes good and bad persons are not easily distinguishable/distinguished. Good or evil, noble or mean may look the same to some people. One needs to be careful and vigilant in distinguishing such people in their life lest, they should repent later!

Kashmiri Proverb # 77

KARIM NANAHWOR
(OR, 'NANAHWOR NAAV')

करीमु ननुवोर
(या, 'ननुवोर नाव')

كريم ننوور (يا،ننوور ناو)

Meaning: KARIM = Name of a person

NANAHWOR = Barefooted.

Barefooted Karim*.

*Name of a person

Usage: The proverb is based on a real time story of a person called, 'Karim' in Kashmir, who one day was seen walking without shoes. The people called him 'Barefooted Karim'. Although, always afterwards, he wore nice shoes, yet the people continued to call him so till his death.

'Give a dog a bad name and hang him', is an English Proverb with a similar meaning, said by Dale Carnegie in 18th century. It's meaning is that if a person's reputation has been besmirched, then he/she will suffer difficulty and hardship throughout life.

It is very difficult to lose a bad reputation even if it's unjustified.

A bad reputation/stigma gets stuck to a person as a wet rag ('ADER ZET' 'अदर ज़ट'), no matter how hard one may try to prove to become otherwise.

Kashmiri Proverb # 78

KHARAS GOR AAPRUN RAAVI DOH

ख़रस गोर आपरुन रावी दोह

خرس گور آپرون راوی دوه

Meaning: KHARAS = Donkey

GOR = Gur/Jaggery

AAPRUN = Feeding

RAAVI = Lost/Ruined

DOH = Day.

To feed the donkey with jaggery shall waste the day.

Usage: It is the height of optimism for a person to waste a whole day, feeding his donkey with jaggery, hoping that the animal might turn out to be wise, and sweet in its demeanor, not realising that it is an exercise in futility.

Indian lore is replete with adages which convey similar messages such as the wastefulness of speaking words of wisdom to, or argue logically with, an idiot hoping that he would understand your point. We come across such situations quite often in our lives. Attempting to mentor such guys is as unproductive as sowing seeds on a sandy sea shore. End result of such antics is the loss of time and energy.

Kashmiri Proverb # 79

KHENAH MYUTH TAH HORANAH TYUTH

खयन् म्यूठ तु होरन् त्योठ

خینہ میوٹ تہ ہورنہ ٹیوٹھ

Meaning: KHENAH = Eating

MYUTH = Sweet

TAH = But

HORANAH = To return/pay back

TYUTH = Bitter.

Receive sweet, but pay back bitterness.

Usage: The proverb states that it has always been a pleasant exercise for one and all to eat and also enjoy at others' expense. However, paying for such pleasures has often been an unwelcome and a bitter exercise for the folks at large!

One likes to get and enjoy favours, materials, gifts, food items, etc. from others but feels bad in giving back the same. Such people are usually stingy/miser in their dealings and also selfish.

George Herbert, a Welsh Poet, Orator and Priest of 17th century has made a statement with a similar meaning, 'fly the pleasure that bites tomorrow!'

Kashmiri Proverb # 80

KHEWAAN PAANAS TAH THEKAAN JAHAANAS

ख्यवान पानस तु थ्यकान जहानस

خیوان پانس تہ تھکان جہانس

Meaning: KHEWAAN = Eating

PAANAS = Himself/Herself

TAH = And

THEKAAN = Boasts

JAHAANAS = To the world.

Eats himself and boasts to the world.

Usage: The proverb means that whatever a person might eat but, habitually goes around bragging, likely talking tall about what he/she eats which might as well be a humble meal or even no meal at all. Also, a person who boasts about his/her achievements/possessions! Such people are egoist, self-centered and believe in self-praise. They suffer from inferiority complex, need to be taken with a pinch of salt. Most probably, he/she is a selfish and compulsive braggart!

Kashmiri Proverb # 81

KHIDMAT CHHEH AZMAT

ख़िदमत छु अज़मत

خدمت چھ عظمت

Meaning: KHIDMAT = Service

CHHEH = Is

AZMAT = Honour.

Service is honour.

Usage: People of humble means and social standing have, by dint of hard work and commitment to chosen goals, achieved excellence in various fields. History is replete with tales of such people in all walks of life, and include teachers, doctors, social workers, and maestros in various intellectual fields.

For them work is worship, and service to the mankind is an act of piety. As the old saying goes, 'Service to man is service to God' which implies that assistance offered to fellow-beings involving self-sacrifice is synonymous with veneration of God. To love mankind, according to Swami Vivekananda, is to glorify the Almighty. The proverb lends motivation to everyone striving to achieve pre-eminence in their respective fields.

Kashmiri Proverb # 82

KHUR AI AASIH BILKULL SAAF, TOTIH AASANAS HATH PHEPHARAH

ख़ोर ए आसि॒ बिल्कुल साफ़, तोति॒ आसनस हथ फ़ुफ़्फ़र

خور ائی آسیہ بلکل صاف،توتہ آسنس ہتھ پھیفرہ

Meaning: KHUR = Scabby head

AI AASIH = Be

BILKULL = Totally

SAAF = Clean

TOTIH = Still

ASANAS = Have

HATH = One hundred

PHEPHARAH = Pimples.

Even a cleaned scabby head will have hundred pimples on it.

Usage: Reference in this proverb is being made to the one who may have been suffering from scabies of his scalp. But, even it gets treated, there still will remain some traces of the disease (pimples) on his/her head. A similar example goes like 'a crow bathed seven times with soap cannot rid him of the traces of black'!

It is a law of nature which holds good across humans and animals alike.

However, much one may try to change for the good, there always will remain the residual effect/traces of one's past.

Similarly, however great heights/achievements one may rise to, the tell take marks cannot be rid off, the shadows shall always be chasing him/her. Traces of his previous state shall never be wished away, however, hard one may strive.

In Urdu/Hindi, its equivalent is one's 'Zamir' (ضمیر/ज़मीर) or 'Khaslat' (خصلت/खसलत), meaning conscience, nature or trait, which does not normally change with change in one's status/stature.

Kashmiri Proverb # 83

KIJI PEATH KAAJWATH
VILLINJI PEATH VOKHUL

किजि प्यठ काजवठ,
विलिंजि प्यठ व्खुल

کیجی پیٹھ کاجوٹھ،
ولنجی پیٹھ وخول

Meaning: KIJI = Peg

PEATH = Upon

KAAJWATH = Pestle

VILLINJI = Clothes Line

VOKHUL = Mortar.

Pestle upon a peg and a mortar upon a clothes line.

Usage: The proverb states a situation where one tries to place a pestle upon a peg, and a mortar upon a clothes-line. This state of activity naturally will not hold, but will tumble. Both are untenable situations, even to contemplate them.

Also, the proverb means where a person is entrusted with or asked to undertake a task that does not suit him/her capability or temperament. In either case, such an approach is most likely to end up with having a badly organised or rickety system not worthy of a decent organization that has got to be result/demand driven! Hence untenable as the proverb suggests. This could as well mean 'fitting a square peg in a round hole and vice-versa'!

Kashmiri Proverb # 84

KOKRAS CHHAI KUNI ZANG

क्कुरस छय कुनी ज़ना

کوکرس چھے کونی زنگ

Meaning: KOKRAS = Cock

CHHAI = Has

KUNI = Only one

ZANG = Leg.

Cock has only one leg.

Usage: A cock is often seen standing on one leg as if to relax or to test its own balancing skill. After a short while, it drops the other leg and walks away. A rustic simpleton watching the first part of the cock show calls out to his folk to claim that this bird has only one leg! It may be just a banter, to be simply dismissed. Or it may be that the guy is a dunce or a prankster.

The proverb conveys a few latent truths. It reveals the mindset of some people to make others accept the incredible, and betrays their stubbornness to stick to what they have chosen to regard as true. Logic and reasoning are not within their reach. Nor are they amenable to corrections. Such people are misfits in cultured societies and are, by and large, looked down upon and thus, be avoided.

Kashmiri Proverb # 85

KU-LIYAA KA'-MUE HUMU-ROWVE-NAKH? PANNUV MAYVAN

कुल्य कॅम्यू होमु-रोव-नख?
पॅनुन्य मेवन

کولیا کمیو ہمو-رووینخ؟ پننو میون

Meaning: KU-LIYAA = O, Tree

KA-MUE = Who

HUMU-ROWVE-NAKH = Bow down

PANNUV = My own

MAYWAN = Fruits.

'O tree, who made you to bow down?' 'My own fruits.'

Usage: A person, however strong, commanding and disciplined he may be, would sometimes be forced to take a stand against his own will or conscience if a member of his family, society or group takes a different or opposite view due to compulsions known only to him. The strongman relents with the sole intention of taking everyone along. This happens due to the pressures exerted from within rather than without.

Similar examples exist in life, where internal enemies do harm more than outsiders, causing failure and disaster.

Kashmiri Proverb # 86

KUKUR TACHHAAN TAH PUTI HECHHAAN

कक्कुर तछान तु पूतृ हेछान

ککور تچھان تہ پوتی ہیچھان

Meaning: KUKUR = Hen/Fowl

TACHHAAN = Scratches

TAH = And

PUTI = Chicks

HECHHAAN = Learn.

The hen scratches and then pullets learn.

Usage: Scratching the ground is an essential act indulged in by chickens while foraging for foods such as worms, insects and grains lying hidden in the soil. The art of scratching the ground for food comes to the pullets largely by imitating the mother, though a small element of natural instinct may also play a role.

Learning by emulating others is a natural event in the daily lives of both animals and human beings. The right and the wrong are both watched and copied by the young ones. It is, therefore, very important that elders live virtuous lives so that their children grow into ideal citizens.

Kashmiri Proverb # 87

KUN LAGHI NA GAJJI TE

कुन लगि नु, गजि ति

کون لگھی نہ گجھی تہ

Meaning: KUN = Alone/Single

LAGHI = No use

NA = Not

GAJJI* = Earthen hearth

TE = Even.

*GAJJI is DHAAN in Kashmiri (दान or دھان)

Singleness is not good enough even for a hearth.

Usage: Experience tells us that fire in a hearth cannot be ignited with just a single piece of firewood. A minimum of two pieces will be required to set up the hearth. The proverb underscores the merits of group effort in securing success in any endeavour. Collective wisdom of a team scores over that of one or two individuals, however insightful the latter may be. A team always performs better in decision making, fighting against odds, both physically and intellectually, and even in sharing the wrath of failures. The statement 'one plus one makes eleven' is said to be the claim by a jester, but it does highlight the power of synergy explicit in his words and implicit in the proverb under discussion.

Kashmiri Proverb # 88

KUR KUR KARAAN PANANIH GARIH, THOOL TRAAWAAN LUKHANDIH GARIH

कुर कुर करान पननि गॅरि, ठूल त्रावान लूक्हहन्दि गॅरि

کور کور کران پننہ گریھ، ٹھول تراوان لوقھندی گریھ

Meaning: KUR KUR = Crying/Chuckling

KARAAN = Does

PANANIH = Own

GARIH = House

THOOL = Egg

TRAAWAAN = Laying

LUKHANDIH = Another's.

Makes noise in own house but lays eggs in another's house.

Usage: The original proverb with somewhat similar meaning goes like this: 'a deceitful (*badzaat*) hen lays eggs in other's homes' or *'panin kokir nai badh aasaih, bai sindhi ghari kyazi travaie hey thool'*!

This proverb holds good for other animals as well as human beings too. Among human beings, it applies to a person who is devoid of loyalty to his master, family, community, or country, while at the same time he enjoys all the privileges and benefits offered by them even as he is clandestinely in league with the rival group. Such a person may, in course of time, feel disgruntled at home or may quarrel with own relations and go about discussing personal matters aloud in the neighbourhood and in effect washing dirty linen in the public. Such people are selfish and would see only their own interests and would not be trustworthy.

L

LAER KHEWAAN PAANAS TAH DAKAAR TRAAWAAN BEYIS

लॉर ख्यवान पानस तु ड़कार त्रावान बेयिस

لیر خیوان پانس تہ ڈکار تراوان بعیس

Meaning: LAER = Cucumber

KHEWAAN = Eating

PAANAS = Himself

TAH = And

DAKAAR = Belches

TRAWAAN = Throws

BEYIS = Other man.

Man eats the cucumber and belches toward others.

Usage: This proverb is about a cucumber-eating person, who, not only avoids sharing it with friends, but demonstrates his obnoxious habit of belching aloud in their presence. The action reflects the person's lack of respect or regard for the sensitivities of others. By such indecorous act he is exposing a range of negative traits like selfishness, lack of etiquette, rustic upbringing, disregard for others' feelings, wanton boastfulness and penchant to offend others. People with self-respect would try to avoid the likes of such a person.

Kashmiri Proverb # 90

LANTSH BUDAAN TAH PULAHARI VONAAN

लॉछ् बुडान तु पुलुहर वोनान

لنچھ بوڈان تہ پولحر ووٰنان

Meaning: LANTSH[1] = Eunuch

BUDAAN = Gets Old

TAH = And

PULAHARI[2] = Grass Shoes

VONAAN = Weaving.

[1]Eunuchs are known for their unique jesting style as well as for their baritone voice that finds appeal in some folk dances. In their younger days, members of this clan are employed in massage parlours and harems of Nawabs. Some do jobs as errand boys and as escorts to socially upbeat women. Crafty ones are even used by spying agencies.

[2]Pulhar is a footwear, made of wheat or paddy straw, worn by the poor in Kashmir during winter, both for warmth and to avert skidding on icy roads.

The eunuch who got old weaves grass shoes.

Usage: The proverb highlights the plight of eunuchs in their old age when their appeal fades away and are rendered jobless. Many of them are forced to take up low-paid vocations like knitting slippers out of straw.

The proverb is a reminder to middle class people about the sanctity of saving for the rainy day. Fate similar to that of eunuchs could befall people who fail to practise thrift and saving. Such people are often compelled to take up modest employments inconsistent with their calibre and social status. Even the wages might be far from fair. The proverb seems to subtly urge people to develop the habit of saving so that their twilight years could be tension-free.

Kashmiri Proverb # 91

LONCHIH LAMUN

लोंचि लमुन

لونچی لمون

Meaning: LONCHIH = End part of a garment

LAMUN = Pull.

To pull the garment.

Usage: The proverb means to pull an end of a garment of a person at arm's reach from or closer to you, is resorted to in order to draw his/her attention. In Kashmir, it means to pull the garment, asking a person to 'pay up'. Shopkeepers and especially, hawkers frequently lay hold of a man's 'pheran' until he pays for the goods just purchased. This method is a most respectful way to ask for money without knowing others!

In other situations, it may be a romantic activity too, else in a sensitive discussion/debate, may be even to caution a colleague to stay on guard.

The proverb basically means to draw attention of your friend/partner/family acquaintance sitting/standing close by your side without others noticing it.

M

MAAJE GABUR AASUN

माजि गबुर आसुन

ماجھ گبور آسون

Meaning: MAAJE' = Mother's

GOBBUR = Son/Child

AASUN = Is/To be.

To be mother's son/child.

Usage: The proverb means a pampered child, having received both the attention as well as protection all along in his life by the mother. He is never called upon to face challenges resulting him to be a softie/sissy child. Such children are born with a silver spoon in their mouth.

The child is considered to be as a preferred or a 'blue boy' in the family. However, too much pampering may spoil a child and turn him an undisciplined one/a brat, which would be difficult for the family to handle at a later stage.

Kashmiri Proverb # 93

MEDER MEKRAAZ

मदुर म्यकुराज़

مدیر میکراز

Meaning: MEDER = Sweet

MEKRAAZ = Scissors.

Sweet scissors.

Usage: The function of a pair of scissors is to cut, dress, prune or damage anything, it works upon. A pickpocket too works with his/her nimble fingers upon its victim, so also a cheat in the garb of a friend. All these act stealthily and damage upon their victims/prey yet appearing absolutely friendly!

They talk sweet to their victim, all the same proceed with their ill designs.

We call such people using scissors of sugar, but none the less sharp and cutting for all that also are very crafty and selfish.

In every society, there always exist people who are fond of creating feuds just for the fun of it or with a purpose. In Ramayana, the maid of Maharani, Kaikeyi acted as sweet scissors, so also in Mahabharata, Shakuni.

Besides, in workplaces, families, etc., feud creators exist and they are always on the lookout of potential targets. Such people must be avoided.

Kashmiri Proverb # 94

MIA-NYAN KATHAN CHHO-CHE' KARINI

म्यान्यन कथन छ्वचि करनि

میانین کتھن چوچّی کرنی

Meaning: MYA-NYAN = Mine

KATHAN = Sayings/talk

CHHO-CHE' = Bread (Chapati)

KARINI = Making.

Making bread of my sayings.

Usage: This proverb relates to persons who seek and derive advice and directions from others but, would neither act accordingly, nor appear to value the guidance thus received. Such persons try to create the impression that they acted as per their own wisdom and judgement. They consider themselves to be so high in calibre and social standing that their ego would not permit them to be seen as seekers of advice. Of course, some of them may, by way of compliance with certain procedural norms, formally seek suggestions from others but, would simply ignore them to keep their ego unhurt. It is here we say: 'Mia-nyan Kathan Chho-che' Karin'. It is as if their motto is to pretend listening to everyone but act on their own. Such people are ubiquitous in every society.

Kashmiri Proverb # 95

MORDAS CHHIH WADAAN BIHIT, BATAS CHHIH WADAAN WUDANIH

मोरदस छि॒ वदान बिहित, बतस छि॒ वदान वो॒दनी॒

موردس چھی ودان بہیت،بتس چھی ودان وودینی

Meaning: MORDAS = Dead

CHHIH = For

WADAAN = Weep

BIHIT = Sitting

BATAS = Food/cooked rice

WUDANIH = Standing.

Sit and weep over dead, but standup for food.

Usage: It is customary to mourn the death of a kin or a friend, sitting around the dead body and bowing down our heads. Once the mortal remains are disposed of, the loss in material terms will start staring at the members of the family. The depletion of financial resources following the breadwinner's death would take centre stage in the family's worry and concern. The tenor of the mourning would accordingly change from one of loss of life to loss of financial resource. This transformation is figuratively stated in the proverb as mourning in the standing posture, for food!

Sitting and bowing down our heads here convey the expression of respect for the departed soul whereas 'standing', shows the expression of concern about the family's future. The proverb conveys the message that the loss of the kins' livelihood is no less important than the sense of deprivation caused by the death.

Kashmiri Proverb # 96

MOT LAGITH SAALE BATTA KHYON

मोत लांगिथ सालु बतु ख्योन

موت لگّت سالبتہ خیون

Meaning: MOT = Subnormal/Innocent

LAGITH = Pretend

SAALE-BATTA = Feast

KHOYN = To eat.

Feigning subnormal to grab a feast.

Usage: The reference in this proverb is to an imposter who pretends to be sub-normal in many ways, both mentally and physically, to evoke people's sympathy which he manages to exploit for his own advantage. He is well aware of an ordinary man's soft corner for the less-privileged fellow-beings. This guy is so clever and crafty that by the histrionic portrayal of himself as a person wanting in many ways such as being innocent and feeble-minded, earns the goodwill and sympathy from others and thereby gets things done. One must, therefore, be cautious while dealing with such people and be not easily swayed by their feigned innocence. One can find such tricksters in all walks of life.

Kashmiri Proverb # 97

MUGAL DISHIT GATSHIH PHARSI KHASUNI

मौगल डीशित गछि फॉरसी खुसुन

مغل ڈیشیت گچھی فارسی خصون

Meaning: MUGAL = Moghul (invaders)

DISHIT = On seeing

GATSHIH = Able to

PHARSI = Persian language

KHASUNI = Speak.

On seeing a Moghul, one should be able to speak in Persian.

Usage: Upon encountering a Moghul, one must be able to speak in Persian language, the Moghul's own mother tongue, so that he/she clearly understands the views and feelings you harbour.

One needs to be *'au fait'* (a French expression) to be completely familiar with details of the subject matter under discussion with the concerned parties. This becomes all the more important while discussing and negotiating diplomatic, political, legal, and scientific matters. For that, one needs to do sufficient homework and be *'au fait'*.

Kashmiri Proverb # 98

MULAN DROT TAH PATRAN SAG

मूलन द्रोत तु पुत्रन सग

مولن دروت تہ پترن سگ

Meaning: MULAN = Roots

DROT = Sickle

TAH = But

PATRAN = Leaves

SAG = Watering.

Sickle to the roots and water to the leaves.

Usage: The proverb underscores the futility of a person's effort in tendering the leaves of a plant even as he mindlessly destroys its roots, inevitably causing the death of the herb. On the face of it, the proverb seems to highlight the failure of wrong priorities in our daily lives. In our anxicty to attain quick success in all endeavours, we tend to employ shortcuts, without envisaging the factors that could ensure sustainable benefits. Here the character in the proverb is eager to enjoy the floral abundance of the plant, but fails because he cares little for the roots. One is reminded of a Malayalam proverb on 'manuring the leaves' which conveys the same thought.

An implied message emerging from the proverb is the sustainability of the root over that of leaves. History is replete with episodes of despotic rulers trying to destroy people's roots in tradition and faiths in order to gain control over their minds, and plant new ideologies in their midst. The reality in the Indian context has been that the tyrants used the sickle but failed to sever the roots. And watering of leaves went on uninterrupted!

Kashmiri Proverb # 99

MYANI GUREA NE LEADH LAAER

मयानि गुरि न॒ लथ्दु लयुर

میانی گوریہ نہ لید لیر

Meaning: MYANI = My

GUREA = Mare

NE = No

LEADH = Faeces/Shit

LAAER = Stuck

My mare has no shit stuck (to its buttocks).

Usage: It may appear to be the height of punctiliousness for any man to claim that his mare can't stink, because poop does not keep sticking to its hind end. But the truth is that the person just feels proud of being clean, honest, blemish-free and carries a good image in the family, society and workplace. People of this kind have the right to take pride in their accomplishments and walk tall, wherever they are. None can belittle them nor cast aspersions.

N

Kashmiri Proverb # 100

NAAGAH GAADAH, WUCHHANIH HALAAL TAH KHENIH HARAAM

नागु गाड़, वुछनि हलहल तु ख्यनि हराम

ناگھ گاڑھ ووچھنیہ حلال تہ خینی حرام

Meaning: NAAGAH = Spring (here, a sacred one)

GAADAH = Fish

WUCHHANIH = To look at

HALAAL = Lawful

TAH = But

KHENIH = To eat

HARAAM = Unlawful.

It is legitimate to look at a fish in a sacred spring but unlawful to eat.

Usage: In India, from time immemorial, places of worship have been constructed in and around water bodies (springs, rivers, ponds, etc.) that abound in fish of a wide range of species. These are reared with care and are revered as divine creatures. Their aquatic frisking and frolics are pleasant to witness.

Similarly, the nature has bestowed upon us several beautiful bounties in the form of non-aquatic animals too that are meant to be enjoyed through our four senses such as sight, touch, smell and hearing. As if to preserve such bounties, even wild animals have been placed on a pedestal of sanctity particularly by the Hindu religion. Snakes, tiger, lion, monkey, etc., which are as revered as they are feared, belong to this group. We need to appreciate them without disturbing or harming them in any manner. A great saying, 'touch not, taste not, handle not', conveys similar commands and insights.

Kashmiri Proverb # 101

NAAR DHRAV SOUUN AASUN

नारु द्राव स्वन आसुन

نار دهراو سون آسون

Meaning: NAAR = Fire

DHRAV = Come out

SOUUN = Gold

AASUN = Becomes/Is

To become gold after passing through the fire.

Usage: The proverb states that to get pure gold, it has to go through process of melting in a crucible. Thus, 'gold come forth from the fire'!

Similarly, to achieve mastery/proficiency of any field, be it art or craft, one needs to undergo rigorous training courses. However capable a person might be, in modern day ever improving/evolving techniques, refresher courses would add lustre to the quality of expertise.

This proverb also holds good in sports, where one is put under rigorous trainings to excel in their respective fields. Even to make high quality wood products, the raw wood requires to be seasoned first by exposing it to extreme temperatures and humid conditions for a specific period.

Kashmiri Proverb # 102

NAH GAMIH DOZAKH, NAH GAMIH JANNAT

नॅ गमि दोज़ख, नॅ गमि जन्नथ

نہ گمیہ دوزخ،نہ گمیہ جنت

Meaning: NAH = Neither

GAMIH = Worried

DOZAKH = Hell

JANNAT = Heaven.

Not worried, hell or heaven.

Usage: The proverb states that the person is carefree and does not worry over whatever happens to him or others around. He neither feels concerned nor shows inclination to take any responsibility even where it is needed. Such characters habitually take everything in their stride, be it sweet, sour or bitter. Nothing fazes them and by nature they are a happy-go-lucky tribe and are good natured, easy to deal with, and could be qualified as 'malleable and ductile'. They bode ill will for none and malice is beyond their comprehension.

Kashmiri Proverb # 103

NAM AI WUTHIH TAH MAAZAS DAG, MAAZ AI WUTHIH TAH NAMAS DAG

नम हय व्यथि तु माज़स दग, माज़ हय व्यथि तु नमस दग

نم ائ ووتهیہ تہ مازس دگ ،ماز ائ ووتهیہ تہ نمس دگ

Meaning: NAM = Nail

AI WUTHIH = If rise

TAH = There

MAAZAS = Flesh

DAG = Pain

MAAZ = Flesh

NAMAS = Nail.

If the nail grows in to the flesh, there is pain in the flesh and if the flesh grows over (the nail), there is pain in the nail.

Usage: Flesh and nail are attached to each other in somewhat the same way as the bone and the flesh. In each pair, the members appear to be complementary to each other in a way they cannot stay separate. A parallel can be found in the bond among members of a well-knit family in which parents and the children form a closed group where mutual tolerance and interdependence has got to co-exist. The entire family gets upset if anyone gets physically indisposed or behaves in an unbecoming manner disturbing the equilibrium, to the detriment of all.

Maintenance of harmony also demands acceptance of each other's weaknesses and proclivities. The exhortation 'love me, love my dog', attributed to St. Bernard of Clairvaux who used this idiom in a sermon, carries the same message. If you love someone, you must accept everything about him, even his faults, much like the flesh-nail combo.

Kashmiri Proverb # 104

NAMI-DAANAM CHHUI RAAHAT-I-JAENEE

नमी-दानम छुइ राहत-ए-जॉनी

نمی دانم چھوئی راحۃ جینی

Meaning: NAMI-DAANAM = I don't know

CHHUI = Is

RAAHAT = Peace

JAENEE = Life.

Ignorance is peace of mind.

Usage: The proverb is a reminder of a practical reality that by remaining unaware of an unpleasant fact or event, we will not be troubled by it. This goes in line with an old saying: 'know not anything about anyone or anything, and you shall preserve your peace of mind'. The same sentiment also echoes in the words: 'the lesser one knows, the sounder one sleeps.' All these sayings seem to endorse a simpleton's belief that ignorance is bliss!

But can ignorance be always blissful? Obviously not. There are two situations where ignorance is not an asset: (i) lack of knowledge about potential dangers around you and (ii) ignorance about the existence of laws. Both will drive you eventually to distress!

Kashmiri Proverb # 105

NANGAS NENDER PRANGAS PYAT,
SAVIS HAERRAPAVIS PYAT

ननगस नऽन्दुर प्रनगस प्यठ,
सॉविस हेरुपॉविस प्यठ

ننگس نیندر پرنگس پیٹھ،
سویس ہیرہ پویسپیٹ

Meaning: NANGAS = Naked

NENDER = Sleep

PRANGAS = Decorated Bed

PYAT = On

SAVIS* = Valuable

HAERRAPAVIS = Steps of Staircase.

*A valuable item or a person who is wealthy (SAVIS...origin Iran).

Naked man sleeps on the decorated bed while a wealthy man sleeps on the steps of a staircase.

Usage: This proverb makes an oblique reference to a man who owns nothing (nothing to hide?) but, for the same reason, is able to enjoy sound sleep on a cozy, decorated bed. He is carefree, has nothing to worry about, and his mind is at peace. His antithesis is a person who owns wealth but keeps perpetually struggling to safeguard his fortunes. He prefers, therefore, to sleep on the staircase leading to the storehouse of his treasure! The person does so in order to keep vigil, looking out for a likely intruder or a thief, throughout the night.

The proverb is a metaphoric illustration of the well-known fact that wealth and luxury, sought after by every man, do confer a sense of insecurity on the recipient. The proverb thus seems to hint at the dictum: 'riches entail misery; stay poor and sleep!'

Kashmiri Proverb # 106

NEKO, NEKH KAR TAH BADH LABIH PAANAI

नेको, नेखु कर तु बडि लबि पान्य

نیکو نیک کر تہ بد لعبہ پانے

Meaning: NEKO = Oh, good man

NEKH = Good

KAR = Do

TAH = And

BADH = Wicked

LABIH = Will get fruit

PAANAI = His/herself.

Oh, good man, do good, the wicked shall get the fruits.

Usage: The proverb urges the do-gooder to continue with his righteous deeds undaunted by the presence of adversaries and ill-wishers who may keep placing hurdles on the way. It is in the way of nature to bestow fitting reward for good deeds while the evil doer will be condemned to face punitive hardship. Law of Karma says if you dedicate life to doing good, you will be rewarded. In other words, 'everything you do comes back to you'. The law applies to both good and evil, in conformity with the English proverb: 'as you sow, so you reap'.

Kashmiri Proverb # 107

NURAH BUTHIS CHHUH GATSHAN
SURAH BUTH YATIMAS

नूर बुथिस छु गछान सूर बुथ यतीमस

نوره بوتهس چهوه گچهان سوره بوتھ یتیمس

Meaning: NURAH = Bright

BUTHIS = Face

CHHUH GATSHAAN = Becomes

SURAH = Ash-colour

BUTH = Face

YATIMAS = Orphan.

A bright face becomes ash-coloured on being orphaned.

Usage: This proverb makes a veritable assertion that a bright and beautiful face of a person turns ashen upon learning that he has become an orphan. The face loses its sparkle and becomes disheveled. Turning into an orphan is utterly devastating.

For all practical purposes, poverty can be seen as a state synonymous with that of being an orphan. If a person, for any reason, suddenly turns poor, he develops a haggard look, almost in a jiffy.

Poverty is always seen by everyone as a curse. Once upon a time, a son asked his father: 'what is wrong in poverty?' The father replied: 'really nothing, son, but get rid of it as fast as you can!'

To be orphan is a great curse and may God protect the parentless!

O

Kashmiri Proverb # 108

OOR-ZUVE DUR-KUTH GAYI BAYED DAULAT

ओर-जुव दोर-कोठ, गॉयि बॅड दौलत

اور-زوو دور-کوٹھ،گئی بڈھ دولت

Meaning: OOR-ZUVE = Healthy

DUR-KUTH = Strong Knees

GAVI = Are/Is

BAYED = Big

DAULAT = Wealth.

Healthy and strong knees is a big wealth.

Usage: This proverb is uttered as thanks giving, usually a reciprocated blessings/wishes made by an individual (especially an senior/older person) to a younger person in the family/society. The person acknowledges it through the blessings, 'may the Almighty bestow you with a good health and strong knees', that being the real assets in real life. As said, 'health is wealth!'

In Kashmir, this proverb is also uttered as a blessings to any service provider, helper, assistants, etc. in the family/society/workplace.

Kashmiri Proverb # 109

PANANE HACHIH CHHEH BAHAH TRACHIH

पननि हचि छे बाह त्रेचि

پننی ھچیہ چھ بھاہ ترچیہ

Meaning: PANANE = Own

HACHIH = Harvest

CHHEH = Is

BAHAH = Twelve

TRACHIH = Trak*.

*Trak is a measure of grain, equivalent to 4.43 kg.

One's own harvest weighs twelve traks (heavy).

Usage: One's own harvest should be sufficient and satisfying, no matter how small it is. The proverb seems to highlight the general notion that one should hold on to one's own possessions, whether one is rich or poor, and should sail through times of adversity. One should trust and count on one's own resources rather than rely on others' mercy. As wise men have said, it is only your own muscles and bones that carry your weight.

The proverb 'a bird in the hand is worth two in the bush' carries a somewhat similar meaning. What you already possess is more valuable than a mere promise of gaining something much greater. You should be contended with what you possess rather than fall a prey to greed. The produce from your own labour is sweet!

Kashmiri Proverb # 110

PANANEV CHHUH NAH PAIGAMBAR MOUNUMAT

पनन्यव छु न पैगम्बर मोनमुत

پننیو چھوہ نہ پیغمبر مونوموت

Meaning: PANANEV = Own people

CHHUH NAH = Not accepted

PAIGAMBAR* = Prophet*

MOUNUMAT = Accepted.

*Prophet, here also means: knowledgeable, wise, expert, etc.

A prophet is not accepted by his own people.

Usage: The proverb means that 'familiarity breeds contempt'. The English writer, Geoffrey Chaucer was the first to use this expression in 1386 in his work titled, 'Tale of Melibee'. This applies to and for all, be it men as well as material! One's mother/wife may be a queen of beauty, possessing all desirable/appreciable/conceivable attributes in town but, for the child/husband, she is just a mother or wife. In economic terms too, we call it 'dwindling utility'. May be stretched in any direction, best fruit in town, for its gardener assumes a mundane value!

In Hindi, one comes across a proverb with a similar meaning: *gar ki murgi dal ke barabar* (गर की मुर्गी दाल बराबर)!

No one takes near and dear ones from within family/workplace or close circle seriously on any matter when it comes to suggestions/advices etc.

Self-possessions are always undermined and other's possessions seem better. Sometimes we derive pleasure in possessing things made in foreign countries (China, Japan, USA, etc.), even though these may be of inferior quality.

Also, extensive knowledge of or close association with someone or something leads to a loss of respect for them or it.

Kashmiri Proverb # 111

PANANIH GARUK HAAK-WAAK CHHUI BEYIH SANDIS PULAWAS BARAABAR

पननि गॅर्युक हाख-वाख छुय बेयिसुन्दिस प्लावस बराबर

پننی گروک حاک ـ واک چھوئی بعیسندس پولاوس برابر

Meaning:

PANANIH = Own

GARUK = Here, garden

HAAK-WAAK* = Here, vegetables

CHHIU = Is

BEYIH SANDIS = Another man's

PULAAWAS = Pulaav

BARAABAR = Equal.

*'Haak' ('Saag' in Hindi), is a green leafy vegetable commonly grown and eaten in the Kashmir Valley, also called 'Collard greens' in the West. This vegetable is almost a 'must' dish prepared in every Kashmiri family, like the Dal in the other parts of India.

Vegetables (Haak-Waak) from my own garden are equal to pulaav of another man's house.

Usage:

There is a common saying in Kashmir: 'give a Kashmiri Haak-Batta. He would always prefer to have that over any other dish such as Pulao or other similar delicacies'.

Similarly, the vegetables from one's own kitchen garden, however humble, shall always be valued more than any those grown elsewhere. The fruits raked in with the sweat of a person's brow shall always be tastier and more dependable than what is obtained from elsewhere. One should always pin trust in one's own resources for they form the anchor for one's very existence, and will prove to be sustainable in the long run. In fact the very essence of the Government of India's *Atmanirbharata* (self-sufficiency) philosophy seems to have originated from proverbs of this kind.

Kashmiri Proverb # 112

PANNUN YEZAT TSHU PAANAS TAANY

पनुन यज़थ छु पानस तान्य

پنون یزت چّهُو پانس تانی

Meaning: PANNUN = Self

YEZAT = Respect

TSHU = Is/Rests

PAANAS = Own/Yourself

TAANY = Up to.

Self-respect rests on oneself.

Usage: The respect one earns from the society depends entirely upon how one behaves with others. No man can expect to receive respect on a platter. He has to gain it by doing good work and being helpful, honest, believing in values of life and above all, being a good soul. As wise men have said, you should strive to command respect rather than opt to demand it.

Eleanor Roosevelt had once said: 'No one can make you feel inferior without your consent'. It all depends on your own self how others would treat you.

So, one should avoid situations and actions that may undermine one's self-respect.

Kashmiri Proverb # 113

PANSAH NISHIH CHHUH PANSAH PHATAAN

पाँसस निशि छु पाँसु फटान

پنسہ نشیہ چھو پنسہ فٹھان

Meaning: PANSAH = Paisa (Money)

NISHIH = Near

CHHUH = Does/Is

PHATAAN = Burst out.

Paisa* bursts out of paisa.

*Money

Usage: The proverb is a subtle reminder of an axiom in layman's economics that the more income you have, the higher your rate of returns from investments, and the more wealth you build. It also follows that the poorer you are, the more difficult it is to earn good returns and build your savings. Money makes money' or 'Money begets money'; thus goes an old saying.

All the above maxims point towards one universal reality: the rich get richer and the poor tend to be poorer! In other words social inequality can only grow; it is not amenable to reversal. The issue poses a challenge to the state battling to create an egalitarian society in which the rich-poor chasm is narrowed down. Is it a possibility or just a pipe-dream? Only time will tell.

Kashmiri Proverb # 114

PHIRIT PHERAN TSHUNUN

फिरिथ फ्यरन छुनुन

پھریت پھیرن چھونون

Meaning: PHIRIT = Turning

PHERAN* = Garment

TSHUNUN = Put-on/wear

* 'Pheran' or 'Phiran' is the traditional outfit worn universally by either sex in the Kashmir valley. It consists of two gowns, one over the other. The outer made of cotton for summer and wool for winter. The traditional Pheran extends up to the feet, popular up to the late 19th century. However, a relatively modern variant of the Pheran extends to below the knee level.

To put on a Pheran, inside out.

Usage: This proverb finds its use during a 'blame game', where one party accuses the other for playing foul. The victim instead of accepting his/her guilt throws back the blame upon the former for being the root cause for precipitating such an action! Every society abounds in such people who never accept their fault instead blame the society. Terrorism, being one such current example. For their corrupt mental make-up and/or other ulterior motive, they blame the society proving themselves victim. Similarly, this proverb is used when the person though guilty for having erred attempts to throw the blame at the door of the accuser, thereby extricating himself blameless and clean one.

Kashmiri Proverb # 115

POUNDHI PYAT ZAAMUTT

पोन्दि प्यठ ज़ामुत

پوندھی پیٹ زاموت

Meaning: POUNDHI* = Sneezing

PYAT = On/At

ZAAMUTT = Born.

*Sneezing is a sudden blast of air, with mucus, expelled from the mouth caused by allergy to pollen, mold, dust, etc. Sneezing is believed (by Ancient Greeks, Egyptians and Romans) as a signal from Gods foreboding the future. A sneeze could be either a good or a bad omen, bringing good luck or misfortune, mostly the latter. In East Asian countries, there is a superstition with different interpretations in respect of the number of times one sneezes such as: once brings good, twice heralds something bad, thrice portends love and four augurs a tragedy in the family.

Born at sneezing.

Usage: The proverb states that if a child is born at the place and time when someone sneezes just once, it is not considered a good omen as per the belief prevalent in our society (defined above).

Unfortunately, the family and society put a tag on the child as 'born at inauspicious time (warned by someone's sneeze)'. That haunts the child throughout his life especially when something adverse happens either to him or to others because of his presence.

Though difficult, we should get rid of such irrational and pernicious beliefs and strive to promote a positive mental attitude in our society.

Kashmiri Proverb # 116

PURMUT CHHUH GURMUT

पोरमुत छु गोरमुत

پرموت چھو گورموت

Meaning: PURMUT = Well-read person

CHHUH = Is

GURMUT = Well cut.

A well-read person is like a nicely cut stone.

Usage: In the proverb, 'purmut', translates as 'educated'/'tutored' or 'trained'!

The proverb emphasizes that a well-read/trained person is akin to a nicely dressed stone.

He/she is similar to a sharpened pencil meant to be used as such and may, however, be employed to impart finishing touches to the one not so 'well accomplished'. This being the aim also object of the procedure employed during the various extra training courses.

A value-added product being the aim.

A similar example could be cited in the case of diamond cutting industry. This is the practice resorted to in cutting and shaping a diamond from the stock aiming to produce a well cut diamond.

Kashmiri Proverb # 117

PYAWAL ZEV

प्यावल ज़्यव

پیاول زیو

Meaning: PYAWAL* = Female, recently delivered

ZEV = Tongue.

*Usually used for animals, namely; Pyawal bitch.

Tongue of a recently delivered female.

Usage: It is said that God could not be present everywhere therefore, He created mothers to guard/take care of the newborns. Once, the newborns are in danger, say under an attack, the mother raises a hue and cry, shouting to scare away the foe or the predator and/or seeking attention/help by its yelping. This unceasing use of tongue is defined as 'Pyawal Tongue'!

Any mother, a cow, a bitch or any animal even birds resort to such a behaviour, hence the proverb applies to all living mother species.

Any woman having a habit of using her tongue incessantly, for sharing her own family issues/happenings and not allowing others to speak also, at times imaginative lying is termed to possess a 'pyawal zev'!

Kashmiri Proverb # 118

RAAT WAATUN GANGABHAL TAH PAGAAH NAH YAARBHAL

राथ वातुन गनुबल तु पगाह नु यारबल

رات واتون گنگہبل تہ پگاہ نہ یاربھل

Meaning:

RAAT = Night

WAATUN = Arrives

GANGABHAL* = Gangabhal

TAH = But

PAGAH = Morrow

NAH = Does not

YAARBHAL = River bank.

*Gangabhal is a stream tributary to the Sindh river, a holy lake near the top of Mount Harmuk.

Plans to arrive at Gangabhal at night, but does not get to the landing place even morrow.

Usage: The proverb states that a person plans, in his thoughts, to visit Gangabal (tributary defined above) at night but does not even make it to the nearest river bank at dawn. The allusion here is to people who are always in the habit of building castles in the air but, don't happen to execute their plans, however laudable and well-intentioned they may be. They derive immense satisfaction from discussing even the minute details of their programme but there would be no action on the ground.

The mindset of people of the above kind is often puzzling.

Are they just day-dreamers endowed with prolific imagination but deficient in the will to act? Or, are they just show-masters wanting to impress others with their grandiose plans? It is also likely that they are diffident about succeeding in their ventures and need support and guidance at every step, right from the beginning. Left to themselves, this group of 'thinkers' will rarely turn achievers.

Kashmiri Proverb # 119

RABI KHOUDAS KANIE DENI DARITH

रबि ख्वडस कन्य दिन्य दाॉरिथ

ربی خوڈس کنیی دهنی دهیریت

Meaning: RABI = Mud

KHOUDAS = Pit

KANIE = Stones

DENI DARITH = Throw at.

To throw stones into a mud pit.

Usage: If a person hurls stones into a muddy water pit, the muck would throw up/splash back on his/her own face or clothes. It is always advisable to avoid entering into a conversation with anyone who is intolerant or irritable and shows scant respect for another's point of view. Seeking friendship with such ones would be a futile exercise bound to cause harm rather than fetch any benefit to either. Wise men should keep them at bay.

Kashmiri Proverb # 120

RATSHI KAAMI GATSHINE DOAL DIUN

रुच्रि कामि गछ़ि नु डोल दुन

رچّی کامی گچّهنی ڈول دیون

Meaning: RATSHI = Good/Right

KAAMI = Work/Job

GATSHINE = Don't

DOAL = Postpone/Linger on

DIUN = Give.

Don't postpone/linger on doing good work.

Usage: One shouldn't delay performing an intended task, especially when it is for a good cause. Procrastination doesn't pay. As rightly said by Martin Luther King Jr., 'The time is always right to do what is right'. If the intent is good, do it forthwith; and it is bound to succeed. It is pointless to look for excuses to postpone its performance. At this juncture, one can't help recalling Kabir's Doha:

'Kaal Kare So Aaj Kar
Aaj Kare So Ab.
Pal Mein Pralaya Hoyegi
Bahuri Karoge Kab.'

'Finish tomorrow's tasks today;
Today's tasks right now.
Destruction might befall in a moment,
When will you finish them?'

Kashmiri Proverb # 121

RACHHIS DOH TE' TSHOORAS GAER

रॉछिस दोह तु, चूरस गॅर

رچھس دوہ تہ چّھورس گیر

Meaning:	RACHHIS = Watchman

DOH = Day

TE' = But

TSHOORAS = Thief

GAER = Few moments.

A whole day for a watchman, but only a few moments for a thief!

Usage: A watchman is required to keep vigil all the time, day and night, but it takes only a few minutes for a thief to accomplish his intended task, which could range from mundane acts of picking pockets, roadside robberies, etc., to high-tech thieving of classified information from government departments or corporate offices. The proverb assumes prominence in today's world of cybercrimes which have multiplied in recent years.

All modern crimes can be accomplished in a trice if the plot is well thought out and preparations are made accordingly. Both prevention and detection are indeed difficult in case of such crimes. But that is no excuse for going slow with vigilance. Hawk's eye vision like that of the watchman in the proverb, 24 hours in a day, must be practiced by vigilance agencies to keep in check thieves of all hues and colours.

Kashmiri Proverb # 122

RATH WANDAI TAH PUJ-WAANUK

रथ वन्दय तु पुजवानुक

رتھ وندای تہ پوجوانک

Meaning: RATH = Blood

WANDAI = Offer

TAH = Here, will

PUJ-WAANUK = Butcher's Shop.

Shall offer blood of butcher's shop.

Usage: The person pretends to display affection for and respect to his acquaintance by swearing on the blood of a Butcher's shop, thereby putting nothing worthwhile or valuable of his own at stake. The person puts up a false and deceptive appearance pretending to be innocent but, is full of mischief instead. Such people hide their intent and hence are untrustworthy, though they may look otherwise.

Kashmiri Proverb # 123

SAT BUTHI CHHIS CHANDAS ANDAR

सथ बुथ्य छिस चन्दस अन्दर

ست بوتھ چھیس چندس اندر

Meaning: SAT = Seven

BUTHI = Faces

CHHIS = Are

CHANDAS = Pocket

ANDAR = Inside.

Seven faces are in the pocket.

Usage: A person keeps seven different faces up his/her sleeve and uses them suiting the occasion and the people involved. The person is also called as 'Mr. Smooth tongue', everything to every man/woman. The person prefers the side for gaining favours and in a jiffy, could change the stance to suit the opposite camp. Such people have no compunction in retracting their steps without any feeling of guilt. They lack moral code of conduct, are devoid of any ethics or morality. They follow the principle of 'show me the man and I shall show you the rule book'. They could be likened to chameleons, the garden lizard changing colours depending upon what bark they crawl upon for self-survival from predators. We find such people in all walks of life; workplace, political arena and now perhaps in judiciary system too.

One should try to avoid such people.

Kashmiri Proverb # 124

SAT-TUTE TUI ZAANI BOOMSENI HINZ TOUF

सततुय ज़ानि बुमसुनि हुंज़ टक्फ

ستوت توی زاني بومسینی ہنز ٹوپھ

Meaning: SAT-TUTE = Hoopoe Bird*

TUI = Only

ZAANI = Knows

BOOMSENI = Earthworm's

HINZ = Of

TOUF = Sting.

*Hoopoe (हुदहुद) is a colorful bird found across Africa, Asia (including Kashmir) and Europe, notable for its distinctive 'crown' of feathers.

Only Hoopoe (a bird) can feel the sting of an earthworm.

Usage: When the bird hoopoe tries to feed on the earthworm using its beak, the latter retaliates by stinging the bird where it hurts the most. The proverb highlights the fact that it is only the bird that would feel the severity of the sting and not anyone else. This truth is also conveyed by the more popular saying: 'only the wearer knows where the shoe pinches,' the meaning of which is only too obvious.

It is well understood that a person directly affected by an adverse event alone would be able to feel the agony and stress associated with it. By-standers can only express words of sympathy.

In another scenario, a man in high position, say, a conscientious administrator, may turn into an object of criticism for actions which, in another man's view, may appear inappropriate. However, in reality there may be compulsions which the former alone may be aware of. A critic must get into the other's shoe before jumping the gun to pass judgement about him or his action.

Kashmiri Proverb # 125

SEDDIS HEUL KARI KYAH?
(HEUL KYAH KARI SEDDIS?)

स्यदिस होल करि क्याह?
(होल क्या करि स्यदिस?)

سیدس ہول کری کیا
(ہول کیا کری سیدس)

Meaning: SEDDIS = Straight person

HEUL = Crooked path/person

KARI = Will do

KYAH = What.

What will a crooked person's path do to a straight person?

Usage: The proverb states that none can harm/waylay a simple and straight forward person.

To think and also act in a straight forward manner, without any malice or ego shall definitely be beneficial in the long run than to be crafty and crooked even though such an approach may appear smart for a short while.

To be a straight forward in dealings also exhibits the strength of a good character (of the person involved), thereby earning him/her respect and/or rewards in the society, family, workplace, etc.

Kashmiri Proverb # 126

SEZIH UNGAJIH CHHUH NAH GYAV KHASAAN

स्यज़िओंगुजि छु नु ग्यव खसान

سیزیہ اونگھجع چھو نہ گیؤ خصان

Meaning:

SEZIH = Straight

UNGAJIH = Finger

CHHUH = Is

NAH = Not

GYAV* = Ghee

KHASAAN = Taken up.

*Clarified butter.

Ghee is not scooped up with a straight finger.

Usage: Common sense tells us, in agreement with the proverb, that a straight finger will not be able to scoop out a fluid or semi-fluid substance from a container. A Hindi saying goes thus: *'ghee seedhi ungli se na nikle, tou ungli tedi karni padti hai'*. There is need to employ either a ladle or a bent finger to accomplish the task.

A cynical interpretation of the proverb is that where a straightforward approach has no chance of success, a crooked strategy could be the remedy! And that indeed is the 'mantra' in crime detection where the police employs contorted and cruel ways to extort information from criminals.

Kashmiri Proverb # 127

SHAAND-GANDEI TOTA

शान्द गॅन्ड्य तोतु

شاندگنڈ طوتہ

Meaning: SHAAND-GANDEI = Pillow

TOTA = Parrot.

Pillow parrot.

Usage: The proverb translated verbatim means, 'a parrot on your pillow'. The parrot on the pillow being the wife (could be a lady paramour too), who feeds all details, true as well as untrue, to her mate across while relaxing on a pillow, even charging him for the next day likely feuds!

Also, when son after marriage starts misbehaving with parents, his wife is referred as 'Shaand-gandei tota!'

This is also used to be said for a daughter-in-law (कान भरना) to her husband against her in-laws!

Kashmiri Proverb # 128

SHAMASIU TAL CHHEH GATAH

शम्सु तलु छि गट्

شمسی تل چھیہ گہٹھ

Meaning: SHAMASIU = Candle

TAL = Beneath/Under

CHHEH = Is

GATAH = Darkness.

There is darkness under the candle.

Usage: The proverb states that right under the earthen lamp there is a patch of darkness which persists all the time. Here darkness is symbolic of ordinary people's tendency to neglect what is right under their nose. Such people are often found preoccupied with, and engrossed in the thought of what is happening far away rather than be concerned about events taking place right in front of them.

It is ironical that the space so close to the lamp should remain unlit while the rest of the vicinity is brilliantly glowing. Such a strange irony is manifest in the minds of people who display scant interest in events in their family or the neighbourhood but show unseemly concern over the happenings in which they are in no way connected. The proverb offers a subtle advice to people that they should pay attention to matters close to them particularly within their families and their immediate circle of friends. The Hindi saying: 'Chirag/Diya Ke Tale Andhera' (चिराग़/दिया के तलें अंधेरा) has parallel in the above Kashmiri proverb.

Kashmiri Proverb # 129

SHAWL SHAWL HARRH, TOONG VIZE' KUNEE

शाल शाल हारय, टुंगि विज़ि कुनी

شال شال ہرہ ،ٹونگ ویزے کوني

Meaning: SHAWL = Jackal

HARRH = Quarreling

TOONG = Howl

VIZE' = At

KUNEE = Together.

Jackals keep quarreling, but howl in unison.

Usage: Intra-group rivalries and feuds are common among human beings as well as amid flocks of animals, seen on a daily basis. Individuals may keep themselves engaged in skirmishes but when a situation arises compelling them to fight a common enemy, they forget their internecine conflicts, and resolve to confront the adversary unitedly.

Among humans this happens right across political parties, families, dynasties, States and countries. The spectacle is most visible in the animal kingdom. The dictum 'blood is thicker than water', which has a similar connotation, stands as the law of nature. The saying seems to hint that familial ties and loyalties will always be stronger and more enduring than the bonds of friendship.

Kashmiri Proverb # 130

SHISTARAH CHHUH SHISHTARAS TCHATAAN

शॅसतुरुय छु शॅसतुरस च्टान

شیشتره چھو شیشترس چٹان

Meaning: SHISTARAH = Iron

CHHUH = Is

SHISHTARAS = Iron

TCHATAAN = Cut.

Iron is cut by iron.

Usage: The proverb literally means, only iron can cut iron.

For ensuring desired results in all pursuits we need to take hard decisions and adopt mighty strategies while grappling with formidable problems enroute. Similarly in debates, one has to counter sharp arguments from your opponent with equally incisive counter-offensive. By far the best strategy to win is to beat the opponent at his own game. We all know that in a cut-throat business of marketing of any product, one agency may attract customers by offering lavish discounts but could get beaten at its own game at the hands of the competing firm that may offer better discounts! There are also other sayings which convey similar meaning, as for example, 'diamond cuts diamond' and 'set a thief to catch a thief'.

Kashmiri Proverb # 131

SHRUGUI CHHU DHRUG TAH DHRUGUI CHHU SHRUG

श्रोगुय् छु द्रोग तु द्रोगुय् छु श्रोग

شرگوی چھو دھروگ تہ دھرگوی چھو شروگ

Meaning: SHRUGUI = Cheap

CHHU = Is

DHRUG = Dear/Expensive

TAH = But

DHRUGUI = Costly

A cheap item will prove expensive but an expensive one, cheap.

Usage: Any article purchased from the market must possess attributes justifying the price paid for it. At the same time the marketability of any article will depend upon its quality and price. An intelligent buyer would prefer to pay a little more and take home a superior quality article rather than settle for a cheaper one of doubtful merit.

It is but natural for markets to be swamped with goods widely ranging from very poor to top-notch in quality and efficiency, with proportionately different price tags. An impulsive buyer would fall for the cheap article which may perform poorly and may even fail to function altogether. Electrical goods are the best examples! The aftermath of such a 'cheap' purchase is the need to make another purchase of the same article, soon after. The result is that the person incurs a high nett expenditure. The 'cheap' indeed turns out to be 'costly' in the end!

Similarly, an expensive item may turn out to be 'cheap' as it is likely to deliver more than its value in the long run, due to its reliability and longevity.

Kashmiri Proverb # 132

SORAH RAG MELIH TAH, WORAH MELIH NAH

सोरह रग मेलि तु,
वोरह मेलि न

سوره رگ میله تہ،
ووره میله نہ

Meaning: SORAH = Pig

RAG = Vein

MELIH = Match/Show affection

TAH = But

WORAH = Step (child)

NAH = Not.

Veins of affection run in a pig, not in a step child.

Usage: This proverb revolves around a mother, being the kingpin of any brood. A sow can deliver a litter up to 20 piglets in one delivery, that naturally were fathered by more than one male. The young ones would develop and grow in cohesion in complete harmony, belonging to the same mother's vein.

There naturally occurred the matching of the vein.

In comparison among humans, more often or normally, the siblings belong to a single father, whereas the mothers may/could be different thus, not the products of the same vein. Here lies the difference as veins do not match thus, the origin of this proverb, 'there may be vein of affection in a pig, but not in a step child!'

Kashmiri Proverb # 133

SORUI CHHUH DUR, MARUNI OTT CHHUH NAZDEEK

सोरुइ छु दूर, मरुनुय ओत छु नज़दीक

سوروی چھو دور، مرون اوت چھو نزدیک

Meaning: SORUI = All things

CHHUH = Are

DUR = Far-off

MARUN = Death

OTT = Only

NAZDEEK* = Near.

*Here, 'near' means inevitable.

All things are far-off, only death is near.

Usage: The proverb states that death happens to be under your own feet, chasing you as your own shadow ever-ready to pounce upon you. Whereas, everything else happens to be far away!

Also, it means that once born, death is the only thing which is certain/assured, the rest is hard to predict/contemplate.

'Death'.. the only thing inevitable (near) in life, no matter how hard one may try.

In the midst of life, we are in death! Or, all things are far-off, but death is well-nigh at short distance, which can happen any moment!

Kashmiri Proverb # 134

SUMIS SUM NAYAMAT TAH BE-SUM QAYAMAT

सोमिस सोम न्यामथ तु ब्यसोम क़यामथ

سومس سوم نیمت تہ بیسوم قیامت

Meaning:
SUMIS SUM = Like with like

NAYAMAT = Blessing

TAH = But

BE-SUM = Unlike

QAYAMAT = Miserable.

Equals are blessed while unequals are condemned/damned.

Usage:
The essence of this proverb is contained in our daily experience that birds of a feather flock together but, birds of dissimilar feathers tear into one another. For a harmonious life together, a married couple should ideally be of the 'same feather'. Parity in intellectual, emotional and social standing will be an asset in married life. Chances of marital bliss are more if the partners are equals as otherwise one of them might develop inferiority complex that may tend to weaken the bond.

Equality notion also plays a role in friendship among people in general. Informal friendship groups of elders in public gardens are ubiquitous in the country. Even within each group the intimacy is stronger among individuals with similar backgrounds. All this tends to lead us to the conclusion that equals feel blessed as indeed stated in the proverb.

One is reminded of a Persian proverb:

Kund Hamjins Baaham Jins Parvaaz

(कुंद हमजिंस बाहम जिंस परवाज़)

(کند ہم جنس باہم جنس پرواز)

which also literally means 'Birds of the same feather flock together'.

Kashmiri Proverb # 135

SUNAH SUNZ SHRAAKH, NAH WAAR THAWANAS TAH NAH WAAR TRAAWSNAS

सौनु स्नज़ शराख़, नु वार थवनस तु नु वार त्रावनस

سنسینز شراخ نہ وار تھونس تہ نہ وار تراونس

Meaning: SUNAH SENZ = Golden

SHRAAKH = Knife

NAH = Neither

WAAR = Fit

THAWANAS = To keep

NAH = Nor

TRAAWSNAS = To throw away.

A golden knife is neither fit to keep, nor to discard.

Usage: The proverb states that possessing a golden sword/knife makes the owner extremely uncomfortable.

Possessing and keeping a precious item made of gold, lands the owner vulnerable, physically insecure for he needs to keep a constant vigil lest, it should get stolen by the thieves. And parting with a precious item, to which one could even be sentimentally attached happens to be an unwelcome suggestion. Either case, it is a damn difficult decision to be taken!

Also in life, one could come across many such occasions/ examples, where there could be a dilemma for a person to decide to retain/maintain any item/relationship or part with it (to have it or not to have it?)!

Kashmiri Proverb # 136

SUTSHAN DAPAAN PANAHDAWIH 'SARI CHHIH GAMUTI AKI NAAWIH'

सुच्रन दपान पन्
दावि, सॉरी छि गॉमुत्य अकी नावि

سیچین دپان پنہداوی - سری چھیہ گموتی اکي ناویہ

Meaning: SUTSHAN = Needle

DAPAAN = Telling

PANAHDAWIH = Piece of thread

SARI = All

CHHIH = Are

GAMUTI = Going

AKI = One (here, same)

NAAWIH = Boat.

Needle says to the piece of thread: 'We both are in the same boat.'

Usage: A sewing needle and a piece of thread together form a complete unit to perform a worthwhile task. Individually, the two possess no value or utility; in fact they are incapable of accomplishing anything. The two have got to act as a pair, and work in unison, to be of relevance. Realizing its status as an entity without utility when alone, the needle in the proverb cries out in despair to the thread: 'We are in the same boat.'

The proverb seems to glorify matrimonial partnership which enables man and woman to work together for a common goal and win. Living alone is largely bereft of this charm, as indeed felt by the needle and thread remaining idle in their own domains.

Kashmiri Proverb # 137

SYEUD SAADAH CHHUH SHAHZAADAH

स्योद साद छु शहज़ाद

سعید ساده چھو شہزاده

Meaning: SYEUD = Plain

SAADAH = Simple

CHHUH = Is

SHAHZAADAH = Prince.

Plain and simple man is a prince.

Usage: A simple and straight forward person, in today's parlance could also qualify as dim-witted one, having no thorns in his crown. Such people have nothing to worry about and shall always sleep like a prince quiet and comfortable in his well-padded bed!

It is also said that 'uneasy lies the head that wears a crown' or 'more brains leads to restlessness'. It is believed that at times, being over smart/clever and intelligent brings with it ego, arrogance, selfishness, greed, etc. which in the long run could be harmful and lead to misery giving sleepless nights causing discomfort to the person. Thus, a simpleton, though may apparently look a dud to others, turns to be more happy go lucky!

T

Kashmiri Proverb # 138

TATISUI KATAS WASIH MUSLAH

तत्यसुय कट्स वसि मुसलु

تتیسوی کٹس وسیع موصلح

Meaning: TATUSUI = Warm

KATAS = Sheep

WASIH = Come off

MUSLAH = Skin.

Skin will come off from the warm sheep.

Usage: Butchers flay the sheep immediately after slaughtering it, for if the flesh were left to get cold, the skin would come out only with difficulty. In a general sense this could mean that no time should be lost to begin action, once it is known that the appropriate time has arrived.

Timing of any operation becomes paramount to ensure the best results. The saying 'stitch in time saves nine' also extols the merits of timely action to clinch favorable outcome in our endeavours. 'Strike while the iron is hot', and 'make hay while the sun shines' are axioms which also urge us to take advantage of a favorable opportunity as otherwise the intended task might get harder much like the belated skinning of the butchered animal.

Kashmiri Proverb # 139

TELI TOSH YELI NOUSH GHAR WAATI

तेलि तोश येलि नव्श गरु वाति

تیلی توش یلی نوش گھر واتی

Meaning: TELI = Then

TOSH = Rejoice/Feel good/Celebrate

YELI = When

GHAR = Home

WAATI = Arrives

NOUSH = Bride.

Rejoice only when the bride arrives at home.

Usage: The proverb cautions the groom's family to rejoice and celebrate only after the bride arrives at her new home (husband's place). In a wider perspective, the proverb seems to advice people to wait patiently till any anticipated victory or achievement is confirmed to have occurred. Only after the news is established beyond any trace of doubt should festivities begin. This caution is justified by the well-known truth that there could be many a slip between the cup and the lip. Even where success appears sure and certain, unexpected events could occur at the eleventh hour negating our expectations. It is wisely said: 'Don't count your chickens before they hatch'.

Kashmiri Proverb # 140

TETHIS LARAS ZAN TSUTANAS KALAH

टेठिस लॉरस ज़न चोटुनस कलु

ٹیٹھس لرس زن چوٹنس کلہ

Meaning:　TETHIS* = Bitter end

LARAS = Cucumber

ZAN = Like

TSUTANAS = Cut

KALAH = Head.

Beheaded like the bitter end of a cucumber.

Usage:　There are two parts embedded in this proverb: 'bitter end of cucumber' and 'beheading' of the same.

In an average cucumber, more so the ones grown on marshy lands, contain a bitter substance. Practice has taught that this can be removed through slicing off the end that connects the fruit to the vine. Followed by putting a few cuts on to the parted surfaces and rubbing them together using circulatory motion. A froth gets collected that needs to be sliced off, couple of millimeters of this end without losing any time in performing this operation.

Hence the proverb, 'finish the evil before it is too late'!

The second part of the proverb (beheading) pertains to the working of judiciary and also the state craft. Earlier in N-W Pathan regions, the rulers had earned fame for their quick dispensation methods, such ones are still in vogue in Yemen and Saudi Arabia. No sooner was the order given 'behead the man' or 'take out his eyes' or 'cut off his nose', then the executioner would leave and perform the cruel deed.

There is a similar legal maxim, 'justice delayed is justice denied'!

This phrase implies that if justice is not carried out right away timely, then even if is carried out later, it is not really justice because there was a period of time when there was lack of justice.

The proverb thus, means 'a speedy punishment'!

Kashmiri Proverb # 141

TSARI CHHUH RAAHAT PANNI THARI-PETH*

चरि छु राहत पनुनि थरि प्यठ

چری چّھُو راحت پني تھر-پیٹ

Meaning: TSARI = Sparrow

CHHUH = Is

RAAHAT = Comforting

PANNI = Own

THARI-PETH = Bush.

*Other versions of the proverb:

'Tsari Chhuh Kend-thari Peth Raahat' or simply, 'Tsari Chhuh Thari Peth'!

The sparrow finds comfort in her own bush.

Usage: The proverb means that the bird/sparrow feels comfortable upon the thorn bush. Or, the bird experiences comfort/safety in its own bush/branch.

Also, it holds good in humans too where one feels comfortable at his/her own place/state and station, no matter how small/bad or humble it is!

A similar saying goes 'East or West, home is the best or most ideal place to be, regardless of its physical condition'!

Kashmiri Proverb # 142

TSUCHIH-WARIH MANZ NERYA ANZ?

च्व्चि वरि मंज़ नेर्या ॲन्ज़?

چوچھ-وریہ منز نیریا انز؟

Meaning: TSUCHIH-WARIH* = Bread

MANZ = Inside

NERYA = Will come out

ANZ = Goose.

*Kashmiri bread/cookie, barely the size of a palm, in native language called 'Telwur' is baked in an earthen tandoor and meant to be used as a snack over a cup of tea. It looks like a donut, but salty in taste.

Will a goose come out of bread?

Usage: Irrationality of expecting a goose to emerge from a pancake is used in this proverb to validate the fact that there ought to be at least a semblance of parity between effort put in and the outcome emerging from every task. Meagre resources could fetch only limited results. However large a pancake may be, it is only just a snack and cannot be made to satisfy a pack of hungry men. To claim that this snack could be blown up to the size of a goose to fill several mouths is to stretch one's imagination too far.

In Kashmir, this proverb is often used to highlight the fact that families struggling to meet their needs have to strengthen resources by suitable means rather than keep longing for a goose to come out of the pancake someday, an improbable event! What is true for a family is equally relevant for organizations too.

Kashmiri Proverb # 143

TSUR CHHUH BE-NOOR

चूर छु बेनूर

چوور چھو بینور

Meaning: TSUR = Thief/Thieves

CHHUH = Is/are

BE-NOOR = Without light.

Thieves are without light.

Usage: The proverb means that a thief, conscious of the fact that he is committing an unlawful act, attempts to ensure that his activity goes un-noticed, does not see the light of the day. He loves darkness because his deeds are evil. It is an established fact that mostly, a sin or unlawful activity is committed in the darkness or during the night. After committing an unlawful activity, such people usually look always worrisome, exuding depressive looks and lose the brightness and shine in their eyes and of their face. It is said that 'face is the index of mind', their activity shows up on their face, hence 'Be-noor!'

Kashmiri Proverb # 144

UN KYAH ZAANIH PRUN BATAH?

ऒन क्याह ज़ानि प्रोन बतु?

عون کیا زانی پرون بته؟

Meaning: UN = Blind

KYAH = What

ZAANIH = Will know

PRUN = White

BATAH = Rice.

What would a blind man know about white rice?

Usage: The proverb is just a plain statement of a simple truth that a blind person cannot appreciate light-coloured rice. We human beings are endowed with the five senses that enable us to identify and admire objects of beauty in this world of variety and diversity. We should forever be grateful to the Almighty for His benevolence.

The blind man alluded to in the proverb exemplifies the whole lot of people who either lack the ability to understand others or are disinclined to use their faculties and taka a glimpse at the merits and goodness of others around. Such 'blind' people find subtle allusion in other proverbs too such as 'Only a jeweller knows a diamond's true worth'; 'भैंस के आगे बीन बजाना' (to play harp in front of a buffalo) and 'a monkey knows not the taste of ginger'. The bottom-line is that for the appreciation of anything of value or substance, there is need for skill as much as for will.

Kashmiri Proverb # 145

UNGLAS PYAT BUNGALEH

ओंगलस प्यठ बोंगलु

اونگلس پیٹ بنگلہ

Meaning: UNGLAS* = Measurement done by using fingers of a hand.

PYAT = Upon

BUNGALEH = Bungalow.

*Linear measurement done by putting 3 fingers together (middle & two adjacent fingers of hand, widthwise), which is approximately 2.00-2.25 inches. The word 'ungal' has been derived from 'ungij', meaning finger!

A bungalow upon an 'ungal' of ground.

Usage: The proverb means that a bungalow is constructed on a patch of land, barely an 'ungal' (explained above) on the ground.

The proverb could be interpreted as having a baseless foundation which does not last for long. At times, considered as a good bargain when 'cheap' is a concern.

When a person builds castles in the air or an organization, government or even in a family making unrealistic plans or hopes for the future or proposes an impracticable project which is bound to fail in the long run. The proverb can also be compared with 'day dreaming'!

V

Kashmiri Proverb # 146

VAAV VACHHIT NAAV TRAAVIN

वाव वुछिथ नाव त्रावुन्य

واؤ وچھیت ناو تراوین

Meaning: VAAV = Wind

VACHHIT = After seeing

NAAV = Boat

TRAAVIN = Pushed into waters.

Sail the boat after paying attention to the wind direction.

Usage: Safety considerations demand that a boat should always be securely anchored at the bank/shore of water bodies when not in use. The vessel should be launched into the waters only after taking stock of the intensity of the wind and its direction. The proverb seems to caution us that we must weigh all pros and cons before launching any new endeavour in which risks are involved and stakes are high. This is particularly important in war like situations and while taking diplomatic or policy decisions etc., which might have wide national and international implications.

It has now become necessary to make a thorough risk analysis as a mandatory step in all new projects and programmes before they are launched. The spirit of the proverb is thus visible all around us!

Kashmiri Proverb # 147

VAAVJI VAAV KARUN

वावजि वाव करुन

واویج واؤ کرون

Meaning: VAAVEJ* = Hand fan

VAAV = To induce air flow

KARUN = To do.

*A hand-held device (a single sheet of a light weight board) designed to be waved back and forth in order to induce air flow for the purpose of comforting the user and also to ward off flies and even for easing pain from a wound.

To fan using a hand fan.

Usage: The proverb seems to highlight the merits of the traditional hand fan that has had its origin in ancient China. In countries of the West, ornamental hand fan was flaunted by ladies as a symbol of aristocracy though it is no more in use today.

Hand fan is very much in vogue in India where people, mainly villagers, use it to combat humid weather. Indian tradition used this device on important guests as if to convey their respect and adulation. In today's environment, however, such a show of courtesy would appear highly artificial and as a naked display of flattery. Such tactics are sometimes resorted to even today, though rarely, for extricating undue or speedy favours from the guest.

In family circles, it is not uncommon to see parents displaying their affection towards the most favoured child through excessive adulation. This act of parents is qualified in Kashmir as 'vaavji vaav karun'.

Kashmiri Proverb # 148

VUTH MAAZRATH KARNI

वुठ माज़रथ करुन्य

ووٹھ مازرت کرني

Meaning: VUTH = Lip

MAAZRATH = Hospitality

KARNI = To do.

To do lip hospitality.

Usage: Literally, the proverb seems to point at people who pretend to be cordial with friends through empty show of hospitality, expressed more by words than by action. Such people might extend invitation with a touch of apparent sincerity, but the guests would arrive at the venue only to see an indifferent host. There is a palpable gap between promise and performance.

The proverb is an equivalent of the common English phrase 'lip service' carrying the implied meaning as an expression of support to, and approval of things proffered but not performed. Those indulging in lip service are ubiquitous in society though their presence is more on display in politics and power centres like the government. Such people commit themselves to accomplishing tasks which do not interest them or beyond the limit of their competence. Promises are made by them to be in the good books of others and be popular. On the ground, however, nothing might materialize.

Kashmiri Proverb # 149

WAATTAL BATWAAR

वातल बटवार

واتل بٹوار

Meaning: WAATTAL = Sweeper/Janitor

BATWAAR = Saturday.

Sweeper's Saturday.

(Sweeper dodging to fulfill the promise.)

Usage: This proverb is based on the real time experience on the work culture of sweepers/janitors, who are supposed to clean/sweep the area/lanes/roads earmarked by their respective Municipal Corporations. The job invariably is not performed by them in time and on lodging a complaint, all kinds of excuses and swear words are given with a curt reply/promise that the same shall be attended to on the following Saturday (being the last working day of the week). Alas! that promise normally is never met. Thus, 'waattal batawaar,' got established as a proverb for the sake of brevity!

Similarly, this proverb holds good in other walks of life, viz; workplace, family, society, friend circle, etc. where persons do not keep their promise of either completing the job assigned or whatever one is supposed to do/perform or pay back/return whatever they owe.

He/she will use all sorts of swear words in convincing you of not been able to do so, keeps on postponing/dodging and promising to do the needful at the earliest.

Hence, 'Sweeper Saturday' gained the currency.

Kashmiri Proverb # 150

ZOUVEE HINDH BAAPAT CHHE ZETT NAALE KADAAN?

ज़ोवि हुन्दि बापथ छि ज़ॅट नालु कडान?

زوو ہند باپت چِّھ،زیٹ نالہ کڑان؟

Meaning: ZOUVEE = Lice

HINDH = For

BAAPAT = Sake of

CHHE = Is

ZETT = Garment

NAALE = Through neck

KADAAN = Remove.

Does one remove the garment for the sake of lice?

Usage: The proverb states that one does not remove or discard a garment (say, a shirt in this case), just because a louse happens to be crawling over it. What is conveyed is that a minor, unexpected and isolated event should not be the justification for dropping a whole host of activities scheduled to be performed in an organisation or in a family. Decision makers in business establishments as well as heads of families must weigh the likely fallout from acts of misdemeanour committed by members in their charge, and try to play down the event rather than blow it up or opt for drastic remedies that may turn out to be worse than the malady itself. The character in the proverb ought to have chosen to fling aside the louse rather than discard his garment altogether! Simple but sensible solutions shall always score over whimsical remedies.

Kashmiri Proverb # 151

ZYADA KATHAN CHHUN SOOD

ज़्यादु कथन छुन् सूद

زیاده کتهن چهون سود

Meaning: ZYADA = More

KATHAN = Talk

CHHUN = Doesn't

SOOD = Interest earned.

Excessive talking doesn't fetch additional dividend.

Usage: There is no advantage in talking more words than what are needed in a conversation. Being lavish with words in formal or informal parleys, would merely lend volume and not value to what you like to say. It is wisely stated: 'If you cannot convey your point in one minute, then you won't be able to do it in a day'. Excessive verbosity will only expose your literary vanity without adding to the substance. It is also likely that you tend to deviate from truth and reasoning in your attempt to stretch the monologue. 'Talk less, and to the point' should be the mantra while voicing your opinions. As Polonius in Hamlet puts it succinctly: 'brevity is the soul of wit'.

* * *

ANNEXURE
Kashmiri Proverbs Vol I

Foreword

Proverbs and phrases are employed to describe situations or phenomena through powerful and colourful analogies. These reflect the richness of the language in question. Every language possesses its own share of such jargon, so does the Kashmiri language. The author has successfully managed to collect 101 proverbs. These have been written in English, Hindi and Urdu explained elaborately, rendering them easy-to-read, understand and use.

Following the compulsive exodus of Kashmiri Hindu community, more so the miniscule Pandits now scattered throughout Bharat, also world over, there exists the probability of their mother-tongue getting lost into oblivion in future generations due to its disuse. Therefore, this book, is an important timely-written contribution and every family must possess a copy; so is my earnest desire and also emphasis. His writings reminds me, and must certainly have him too, the film song of Kabuliwala, '*Ae mere pyare watan, tuj pe dil kurbaan...*' also, the English poem 'Breathes there the man, with soul so dead, who never to himself hath said, This is my own, my native land.' It appears that this effort by him has been the culmination of his intense nostalgia for the years gone-by!

Being a Kashmiri Pandit, scholarship runs through the genes of Dr. Raj Kachru, for he belongs to the progeny of the famous poetess 'Arinmal,' an 18th Century leading Kashmiri Poet, known for poignant poetry. She was married to Munshi Bhawani Dass Pandit Kachru, an erudite Persian Scholar, Poet and a Historian. Dr. Raj Kachru's grandfather (Pandit Srikanth Kachru), in addition to being a professional Civil Engineer responsible for constructing the road to Gilgit in POK, the erstwhile part of J&K State and of 'Mohra Power House,' happened to be a prolific multilingual Penman. It can thus be said that a literary streak runs through the DNA of the family.

The love for his mother-tongue coupled with the love for land has propelled Dr. Raj Kachru to recollect his thoughts and put his pen to the paper. This enthusiasm must have further been accentuated by the gap in space and time having been out of Kashmir for the last over sixty years but for being an occasional visitor. These visits by him must certainly have exacerbated the wounds of separation!

I have known Dr. Kachru for the last 50 years. He has been a product of IIT, Kharagpur and later earned his Ph.D. from MSU, USA. He has worked in almost all capacities encompassing, teaching, R&D, research management and consultancy. It wouldn't be out of place to mention here that nothing has escaped his intellect attention and hawkish eyes! Following his instincts and pursuits, he has been a globe trotter. This book too is a reflection of his enthusiasm, effort and determination. I congratulate Dr. Kachru for his interest and efforts in bringing out this publication.

Sincerely, I wish him success in his endeavour.

Prof. Chamanlal Wakhaloo
B.E(Hons), M.E.(Mech Engg); Ph.D. (Eng. Sc.) L'pool, UK.
Founder Principal, (Erstwhile Govt. Engineering College, Bhopal)
Rajiv Gandhi Proudyogiki Vishwavidyalaya, Bhopal, Madhya Pradesh.

Preface

'What seem to us as bitter trials are often blessings in disguise' – Oscar Wilde.

How true it is, as we talk of Covid-19 pandemic, when our movements were all of a sudden curbed and we were confined within the four walls of a home with hardly any space to stretch our limbs. But, this pandemic turned out to be a blessings, for it gave me sufficient time to stretch my imagination and saunter the memory lanes of my younger days back home in Kashmir, which I had left more than six decades ago. This book is the brainchild of that period.

Once, while I was in one of such pensive moods and talking to my dear nephew Tej Krishen, we were recalling some of the sayings our parents and grandparents used to quote and intersperse during their day-to-day conversations. Some references about the special such sayings cropped up, which in ordinary language are called 'proverbs'. These proverbs are so powerful that they get automatically tucked in the long-term memory of our brains.

Proverbs are wise sayings and gems of wisdom that give advice about life. We may sometimes not understand a big lecture but we understand proverbs very easily because the truth they speak can span the globe. They can also give a greater punch to what is being conveyed. A Panamanian saying goes as, 'A proverb is to speech what salt is to food.' The earliest collection entitled, 'The proverbs of Solomon' which the men of Hezekiah, the King of Judah, copied, came into being about 700 BC, the latest dates from the 4th Century BC. Each proverb is a short, wise sentence from long experiences: the school of the wise and the school of fools. Solomon, the son of David, was said to have written over 3,000 proverbs.

Proverbs do reflect and demonstrate national events, social customs and vices. They are found in all languages and societies like:

'Do good and throw it in the sea' or 'A watched pot never boils.' 'The genius, wit and spirit of a nation are discovered in its proverbs,' said Francis Bacon, the 16th Century great English essayist. Generations have passed but those proverbs are relevant even today.

Talking of our own country, a rich land of diverse languages and cultures, and a cradle of powerful religions does use proverbs developed over the years. Kashmir also stands distinct as it has the flavour of local habits, habitat and culture. What bothered me most was whether these proverbs, packed with valuable truths of life, handed over from generation to generation through word of mouth, would slowly dwindle and vanish from our lives especially, when our future generation is distancing itself from the use of Kashmiri language for the reasons created by the circumstances and the mass exodus from the valley. It is this concern, which prompted me to, at least, document these precious proverbs for the benefit of future generations.

I started jotting down the Kashmiri proverbs, which I could recall from my memory with the help of my nephew (Tej Krishen) and his wife (Jyoti) and have been sharing them with my friends in social network. This book is the culmination of the overwhelming response I received for these posts. I was surprised to notice the keen interest shown by my non-Kashmiri friends too. This compilation has 101 proverbs in English, Hindi and Urdu to ensure better reach. I have given the meaning of each word of the proverb annexed with an elaborate description, interpretation and usage, with illustrative examples, to the best of my knowledge and ability, even though it was not always possible to find the most suitable word that would give the exact meaning. I have used the nearest one.

I hope these proverbs would invoke interesting memories in my Kashmiri brethren. I'm also counting on good reception from those of other regions, for I'm sure they too would recapitulate appropriate proverbs in their languages. I would be delighted to receive feedback from the readers for enriching and improving my own understanding of these proverbs.

Thanks! **Dr. Raj Kachru**

Acknowledgements

It took an immense amount of effort and determination to identify and compile 101 proverbs, which I believe would not have survived so long without the invaluable contributions of a number of incredibly thoughtful and supportive people.

First, I'm greatly indebted to my parents, Smt. Gunwati and Pt. Prem Nath Kachru (a real time Karamyogi) and grandparents, Smt. Veshmal and Pt. Srikanth Kachru (a highly disciplined, spiritual and multilingual penman) for their upbringing, love and blessings.

I wish to express my deep and sincere thanks to my family especially, my wife, Madhu, much appreciated for her love, motivation and encouragement besides, keeping cool and inspiring me especially, during the testing times, we all were going through.

I wish to record my profound gratitude to my two dear nephews, Tej Krishen Kachru and his wife, Jyoti and Sanjay Kachru and my favourite niece, Anita Tiku for the evolution of ideas, identification of the proverbs, setting of the draft manuscript, etc. I, however, got a pleasant surprise to find that how much these guys (especially, Tej) know about our days in the valley.... sometimes turning to a big laughter.

I'm thankful to my respected cousin brothers, Prof. Brij Lal Kaul (UK) and Shri Bansi Lal Kachru, whose encouragement, constructive criticism and suggestions have contributed immensely to the evolution of writing of this book.

I'm highly obliged to my dear friend, Prof. Chaman Lal Wakhloo, a renowned professor in engineering and a founder of many technological institutions, the latest being Govt. Engineering College, Bhopal, which finally, blossomed into a full-fledged university, Rajiv Gandhi

Proudyogiki Vishwavidyalaya, Bhopal. He was kind enough to go through the manuscript and write a Foreword.

I express deep and sincere gratitude to Dr. Ranganathan Ramani, Ex-Director, ICAR-IINRG, Ranchi, who is not only my great friend and ex-colleague but always helpful, whenever needed. He has a brilliant sense of putting right expressions and articulating them in a manner, suitable to the subject. He has been working seamlessly during the last few days in setting the Urdu tying and helping in getting this book published. A big thank you, Dr. Ramani for the timely help.

I have no valuable words to express my thanks but heart is still full of the favours received from every person to the run-up of this publication.

Dr. Raj Kachru

List of Kashmiri Proverbs Vol I

Detailed explanations are available in Kashmiri Proverbs Vol I by Dr. Raj Kachru, Notion Press 2021

Kashmiri Proverb # 01

ANIM SOI, VAVEM SOI LAJIM SOI, PAAN SEI

انیم سوئی،وویم سوئی لجیم سوئی،پان سي

अनिम स्वय, ववुम स्वय लजिम स्वय, पानसुय

Kashmiri Proverb # 02

AN POSHI TELLI YELI VAN POSHE

ان پوشی تیلی،یلی ون پوشی

अन पोशि तेलि, येलि वन पोशि

Kashmiri Proverb # 03

ALLA KULIS BANAVUN TULLA KUL

الہ کولیس بناؤن،تولہ کول

अलु कुलिस बनावुन, तुलु कुल

Kashmiri Proverb # 04

ASAV NA TA, LASAV KITH-KYNI

عسو نہِتہ،لصو کیتھکینی

असव न॒ त॒ लसव किथुकॉन्य

Kashmiri Proverb # 05

AKH DUDE, BEYI MAJI KYUT TOAK

اک ڈھوڈھ بیئی ماجي کیوت ٹوک

अख डुड॒ बोयि, माजि क्युत टोक

Kashmiri Proverb # 06

AANCHAAR NOUT, AKIS HOUT TE BEYIS KHOUT

آنچار نوٹ،اکیس حوت تہ بعیس خوت

आंचारु नोट, अकिस होत बोयिस खोत

Kashmiri Proverb # 07

AKH KARAAN TACHI-BACHI BYAKH DIVAAN VACHI-VACHI

اک کران تچّھی- بچّھی بیاک دیوانِ وچّھی- وچّھی

अख करान तछि – बछि ब्याख दिवान वच्छि- वच्छि

Kashmiri Proverb # 08

AKH VOOKUR TE BEYI TRAKUR

اک وکور تہ بعي تریکور

अख वुकुर तु बोयि त्रकुर

Kashmiri Proverb # 09

BEH-MOND

بہ-مونڑ

बेहु-मॉड

Kashmiri Proverb # 10

BAB'AE NAETHER-TE'-YEMI DAM'AE

بہ نیتھر-تہ- عمی دمہ

बबा नेथुर तु यॉमी दमु

Kashmiri Proverb # 11

BATTA-JINN

بتہ جین

बतु जिन

Kashmiri Proverb # 12

BRARI-ZOON

براری زون

ब्रारि-जून

Kashmiri Proverb # 13

BATTAS PEAAT SUUIN

بتس پیٹ سوئن

बतस प्यठ स्युन

Kashmiri Proverb # 14

BOI GAV KANI, BENIH GAYIH THANI

بوی گو کنی،بینیہ گئی تھنی

बोय गव कॅन्य, बेनि गयि थॅन्य

Kashmiri Proverb # 15

BAUNKUN WACCHITIU CHHOUN-KUN WUCCHHUN

بینکون وچّیتی،چونکون وُچّھون

बोन कुन वुछित, च्रोन कुन वुछ्छुन

Kashmiri Proverb # 16

BATTA TCCHHU BRAAND-KANI HOOND

بتہ چھو ،براند-کنی ہوند

बत॒ छु, ब्रांदु॒-कॅनि हुंद

Kashmiri Proverb # 17

BONI MUHUL TAARUN

بونی موہول تارون

बोनि मुहुल तारुन

Kashmiri Proverb # 18

CHIYAANI KATHI TSHU VAZAN MIYAANI KATHI TSHUNA KIHEEN

چیانی کہتھی چھو وزن، میانی کہتھی چھُونہ کیحین

चानि कथि छु वज्ञन, म्यानि कथि छु नु किहीन

Kashmiri Proverb # 19

TSHOPE' CHHAYE' ROUPSENZ KARAKHAI SOUNSENZ

چھّوپ چھی روپسینز ،کرخی سونسینز

छ्वोपु॒ छय रॊपु॒ सँ॒ज़, करुखय तु॒ स्वनुसँ॒ज़

Kashmiri Proverb # 20

CHHAAN JUMMAH RACHHUN CHHOE BOD GUNAH

چّھان جمعہ،رچھن چھوئ بوڈ گناہ

छानु जुमाह, रछुन छुय बोड ग्वनाह

Kashmiri Proverb # 21

CHHARI DAUD TE' MAHE ADIJ

چری دود تی مھی اڑیج

च्रि द्रोद तु महz अडिज

Kashmiri Proverb # 22

DAN-DHE' KHO-KHHUR HAMAAM GAJE', DANDAV TI GAV BANDAV TI GAV

دندھ خوخُھر،حمام گجھے دندو تی گو،بندو تی گو

दंदु ख्खुर, हमाम गजे दंदव ति गव, बंदव ति गव

Kashmiri Proverb # 23

DAAMB – LAAGUN

ڈھامب لاگن

डांब लागुन

Kashmiri Proverb # 24

DAANDAN KHEYE' PATHHI'J PANNIN KHEYEN MANDCCHH

داندن خیے پتھحج،پنن خیین مندچھ

दांदन ख्ये पतिज, पनुन्य ख्यन मंदछ

Kashmiri Proverb # 25

DULLU-MOUNDUL

ڈھولہ موندل

डुल्लु- मंदुल

Kashmiri Proverb # 26

DULLU BRER

ڈھولہ بریر

डुल्य ब्रॉर

Kashmiri Proverb # 27

DRAAG TCCHALI TI DAAG TCCHALINE

دراگ چّھلی تی، داغ چّھلنی

द्राग च्लि तु, दाग चल्लन

Kashmiri Proverb # 28

DAMAS SEEIT TCCHHUE NAMASKAR

دمس سیت چّھوی نمسكار

दमस सुत्य छुय नमस्कार

Kashmiri Proverb # 29

DOORI DOORI TSHHU MARECHH MAETHAAN, NAZDEEKH EITH TSHHU NAABAD TETHAAN

دورِی دورِی چھو مرچ میٹھان، نزدیک ایت چھو نابد تیٹھان

दूरि दूरि छु मर्च मेठान, नज़दीक़ यिथ छु नाबद ट्यठान

Kashmiri Proverb # 30

ENDRI HUMMAL

اندر ہومل

अंद्र हुमल

Kashmiri Proverb # 31

EKI BAALA KHARUN BEYI BAALA VALUN

ایکی بالہ خارون،بیعی بالہ والون

अकि बालु खारुन, बेयि बालु वालुन

Kashmiri Proverb # 32

FARRI TSHOORAS DAARI KOUND

فری چورس،داری کونڈ

फरि चूरस, दारि कोंड

Kashmiri Proverb # 33

GARI TSHUI-NE VAI NEBRA HAAWAAN TIE; TALAE FAAKAI

گری چّھوی نہ وي،نیبر حاوان ٹائی تلہ فاکای

गरि छुय नु वै, न्यबरॖ हावान टै, तल्लुॖ फाकई

Kashmiri Proverb # 34

GAE'L GAE'L GATSHUN

گیل گئئل گچھون

गल्य गल्य ग॒छुन

Kashmiri Proverb # 35

GAJIE – BRURE

گجی - برور

गजि ब्रोर

Kashmiri Proverb # 36

GHARAS GHAR TSHHUNE VAAT DIWAAN, SHAALAS LOAT ZUUET PAANAS TSHHUS

گرس گر چھونے واٹ دیوان شالس لوٹ زویوٹ پانس چھو

गरस गरु छु नु वाठ दिवान, शालस लोट ज़यूठ पानस छुस

Kashmiri Proverb # 37

HALLEN BAANAN, WUQUIR THAANA HEVEN HEVEE SAMKHAAN

ہیلن با نن ،وُکیر ٹھانہ حیون ہیوی سمخان

हल्यन बानन वुकर्य ठान, हिव्यन हिव समखान

Kashmiri Proverb # 38

HUNE' MAA AIEN LIVAN YUOR

ہونی ما عین،لیون ییور

हून्य मा अयिन लिवनि योर

Kashmiri Proverb # 39

HEADUN GAILUN, PAANAS MAILUN

ہڑون گیلون،پانس میلون

ह्रडुन गेलुन, पानस मेलुन

Kashmiri Proverb # 40

HATA HOANE, KHYATA ZANG

هتیہ ھونیہ،خیۃ زنگ

हतुॱ होनि ख्यतुॱ ज़ंग

Kashmiri Proverb # 41

HERI KHASIN, KHYRE TAYEK

ہیری خصین،خیری ٹیک

हिरि खसुन्य, खिरुॱ टॉक्य

Kashmiri Proverb # 42

HARFAS GAWAH, MENDIS SHAREEKH

حرفس گواہ،مینڈس شریک

हरफस गवाह तु मेन्डिस शरीख

Kashmiri Proverb # 43

HYOR NAI PILLAI, ZANGA ZILAI

ہئیر نئی پیلي،زنگہ زیلي

हयोर नय पिल्लै, जंगु जुलय

Kashmiri Proverb # 44

**KOUS HAERR NE' TSHALI TEHRR KHYET MAT' VANTAS
KHEN KAEIM DRAII BEA NE KANH TSH NE KANH**

کوس ہیر نہ چلی، تحرّ خنئیت مت ونتس کینہ، کیم درائ، بیہ نہ کنہ، چہ نہ کنہ

कुस हुहर न च्रलि, तुहर ख्यथ मत वनतस केंह, कॉम द्रायि, बु न कांह,
तु च्रु न कांह!

Kashmiri Proverb # 45

KESRI TAEL POANE ANUN

کسری تیل پونِ انون

केसरि तॉल्य पोन्य अनुन

Kashmiri Proverb # 46

KATHHAV SEITEE NAKHHA VAALUN

کتھو سیتی نکھ والون

कॉथव सुत्यी नख् वालुन

Kashmiri Proverb # 47

KRINJLIS MANZ POANE SAARUN

کرینجلس منظ پون سارون۔

क्रंजिलिस मंज़ पोन्य सारुन

Kashmiri Proverb # 48

KALLA(SARI) PAYET SEHLAAB EYUN

کہلہ پیٹھ سہلاب ایون

कलु(सॅर्य) पेठ्य सॅहलाब युन

Kashmiri Proverb # 49

LABA KHENI IWAAN

لعبہ خینی ایوان

लबु खेन्नि यिवान

Kashmiri Proverb # 50

LORI PEATT SOROUF TAARUN

لوری پیٹ سوروف تارون

लोरि प्यठ स्वरुफ तारुन

Kashmiri Proverb # 51

LONDON KIN LAHORE GATSHUN

لندن کین لاہور گہچّھون

लंदन किन लोहोर गछुन

Kashmiri Proverb # 52

LEMBBI PHOTMUT PAMPOSH

لمبھ فوٹھموت پمپوش

लम्बि फोटमुत पमपोश

Kashmiri Proverb # 53

LORI DASTAAR THAWUN

لوری دستار تھون

लोरि दस्तार थवुन

Kashmiri Proverb # 54

MOMA DED, BIMAAR GAIEE; KHENI VIZZE, HOOSHYAAR GAIEE

مومہ دید، بیمار گئی خینی ویز ،ہوشیار گئی

मोमु द्यद, ब्यमार गयि; ख्यनु विज़ि हुशार गयि

Kashmiri Proverb # 55

MARTSHEWANGAN KHAAR KHET TI KARNI TASS

مرچھوانگن خار خیت، تی کرنے ٹاس

मरचुवांगन खार ख्यथ तु करुन्य टास

Kashmiri Proverb # 56

MUJE PEAT MILVEIN

موجہ پیٹھ ملوین

मुजि प्येठ मुल्यवेन्य

Kashmiri Proverb # 57

MANTUIS GATSHUN PAANZUWU

منٹس گچّھون پانزو

मंटिस गछुन पांजुव

Kashmiri Proverb # 58

MECHHE DUIN NOON

میچھی دیوں نون

म्यचि दुन नून

Kashmiri Proverb # 59

MATTEV ANE' NOSHA SOTTE DRAII MATSHEI

مہتیو انے نوشا،سوتے درائ مچیی

मत्यव अन्ये नव्शा, स्वति द्रायि मॅचुय

Kashmiri Proverb # 60

MUJI KHYET GAV SARAD

موجہ خیعیت گوو سرد

मुजि ख्यथ गव सरद

Kashmiri Proverb # 61

NAMAS PYATT NOON

نمس پیٹ نون

नमस प्यठ नून

Kashmiri Proverb # 62

NEUTHAS PEATT CHHONG DAZAAN

نیوٹھس پیٹ چونگ دزان

न्योठस प्यठ चोंग दज़ान

Kashmiri Proverb # 63

NAARAS DIMAH NERI HAWAAS KARAA GAEJI?

نارس دیمہ نیری،حواوس کرا گئیجی

नारस दिमाह नरि, हव़ुहास करा गेजि

Kashmiri Proverb # 64

OUN DAAND TSHHU RAVRAAVAAN, SAASSAS DAANDAN VATH

اوّن داند چھّو راوراوان،ساسس داندن وتھ

ओन दांद छु रावरावान, सासस दांदस वथ

Kashmiri Proverb # 65

OUDRE ZETT

عیدر زیٹ

अदुर ज़ॅट

Kashmiri Proverb # 66

PANNIAN SAZAA POUTELEN POOZAA

پنن سزا،پوتلین پوزا

पनुन्यन सज़ा, पोतुल्यन पूज़ा

Kashmiri Proverb # 67

PASHE PEATHHE SHEEN VAALUN

پیشہ پیٹھ شین والون

पशु प्यठ शीन वालुन

Kashmiri Proverb # 68

PHATA-WANGUN

فٹہ وانگوں

फट्- वांगुन

Kashmiri Proverb # 69

PAANAI KHATOS, PAANAI VATHOS

پانی خطوس،پانی وتھوس

पानय खॊतुस, पानय व्थुस

Kashmiri Proverb # 70

POGA KATTH

پوگہ کہٹھ

पोगु कठ

Kashmiri Proverb # 71

PACHHA BARAN HUE KHADDA ROZUN

پچھ برن ہوئے،خڈھا روزون

पचु बरन ह्व खड़ा रोजुन

Kashmiri Proverb # 72

PHIN-PHOK TE' GARDE' AASMAAN

فین‌فوک تی گرده آسمان

फ़न्य-फोख तु गरदिआसमान

Kashmiri Proverb # 73

SATAN YAARBALAN FARENAVITH ANI TRESH HETOOV

سہتین یاربلن فرینویت انی تریش ہینتو

सतन यारबलन फेरुनॉविथ अनी त्रेशि होतुय

Kashmiri Proverb # 74

SHAAL TSHHALIT BHATTHEN LORRI/CHOB

شال چلیت،بیٹھین لوری/چوب

शाल च्ॉलिथ, बॅठ्यन लोरि/चोब

Kashmiri Proverb # 75

SAALAS TSHHU MAZA SAIBE PEAT

سالسی چھو مزہ،سبھ پیٹھ

सालस छु मज़, सबि प्यठ

Kashmiri Proverb # 76

SANIS BUTHIS ITI GANIMAT WUNKENKIS WAQTAS MANZ

سنیس بوتھس اتی غنیمت ونکینکیس وقتس منز

सॉनिस बुथिस यिति गनीमथ वुन्यकेंकिस वक्तस मंज़

Kashmiri Proverb # 77

SONAS MUAL, KANAS TAL'

سونس معل،کنس تل

स्वनस मोल, कनस तल

Kashmiri Proverb # 78

SARAAF GANZARAWVAAN DIYAAR, ATRAAF RAWARAVAAN DOH

سرا فِ گنزراوان دیار، اطراف راوّ راوان دوه

सराफ गंज़ुरावान द्यार, अतराफ रावरावान दोह

Kashmiri Proverb # 79

SOUNTH HAI AAV YESS YUTH DRAAV

سونتھ ہے آوٗ،یس یوتھ دراوٗ

सोन्थ हय आव, यस युथ द्राव

Kashmiri Proverb # 80

SOURF PAKAAN HOL HOL, PAR PANI VAJI KUN SYUD

سرف پکان ھول ھول، پر پني واجی کون سعید

स्वरुफ पकान होल होल, मगर पनुनि वाजि कुन स्योद

Kashmiri Proverb # 81

SHOUNGUN BAH TREKH VATHUN KHAAR

شونگون بھا طریق وتھون خار

शोंगुन बाह त्रख, व्थुन खार

Kashmiri Proverb # 82

TCHHE' KHER, MAE' KYA?

چے خیر، میں کیا

च्चे खॅर, मे क्याह?

Kashmiri Proverb # 83

TRIH TE SEHH' TSHET-JI TE PATTJI SHA-ETT TE BRAITT NAMAT TE MAS-KASIT KHYAMAT HATTH TE BEH GHOSS KHYAT

طرح تی سہہ،چّھتجی تی پتجی شیٹ تی بریٹ،نمت تی مسکاست خیمت ہتھ تی، بیگوس خیت

त्रह त॒ सुह, च्रत॒जी त॒ पत॒जी, शेठ त॒ ब्रेठ, नमथ त॒ मस कॉसिथ ख्यमथ, त॒ बु गोस ख्यथ

Kashmiri Proverb # 84

TSHHALIT TENGUL

چھلیت تینگول

छॉलिथ त्यंगुल

Kashmiri Proverb # 85

TCHHEL CHHEL ZIUN ZAALUN

چھیل چھیل ذیون زالوں۔

छ़ेलि छ़ेलि ज़्युन ज़ालुन

Kashmiri Proverb # 86

THHOKE' PEATT RIKKIN GACHHIN

تھوکہ پیٹّ رگّین گچھین

थ्वकि प्यठ रिकिन्य गछ्न्य

Kashmiri Proverb # 87

TIL-ZAALAI

تیلی ذا لیے

तीलु-ज़ालै

Kashmiri Proverb # 88

TAAB TSHHOE LAAB

تاب چھوئے لاب

ताबस छुय लाब

Kashmiri Proverb # 89

TUZUK BALAI

توزوک بلائی

तुज़ुख बलाय

Kashmiri Proverb # 90

VONTH – VUTSHHUN

ونٹھ وچّھون

वोंथ- वुच्छुन

Kashmiri Proverb # 91

VAN-CHAN YAAREN (OR KULEN) KHUDAISUND SUGG

ونچن یاریں، خدائسوند سگ

वनुचन यार्यन खॊदायसुन्द सग

Kashmiri Proverb # 92

WAGOO TSHHATUN

وگوّ چھٹونّ

व्गुव च्टुन

Kashmiri Proverb # 93

WOUZE-MEO KOTOO GOKH, HAALI-HARAAN

وعذیمیو کتوں گوخ،حالحران

वॊज़मियो कॊतू गोख, हालिहॉरान

Kashmiri Proverb # 94

**YEMIS KANN TEMIS NE SOUNN;YEMIS SOUNN
TEMIS NE KANN**

یمیس کن تیمیہس نہ سونّ، یمیس سون تیمیہس نہ کن

यॊमिस कन तॊमिस नु स्वन यॊमिस स्वन तॊमिस नु कन

Kashmiri Proverb # 95

YED SAEET CHOUP HYUN

یہڈ سیت چوپ حیون

यॊड सुत्य चोप ह्योन

Kashmiri Proverb # 96

YAMAS DEENA ZOOV TI

یمس دینہ زوتي

यमस दीना जुव ति

Kashmiri Proverb # 97

YOUTAAIN POUZ PAZZE' TOUTAAIN AALAM DAZZI

یوتائن پوز پزی،توتائن عالم دزی

योतान्य पॊज़ पज़ी, तोतान्य आलम दज़ी

Kashmiri Proverb # 98

YEM HUET, SUH HOET YEM NA HUET, SUH KHOET

یم ہیوت،سو ہوت یم نہ ہیوت،سو خوت

येम्य ह्योत, सु होत, येम्य न ह्योत, सु खोत

Kashmiri Proverb # 99

YETH LATSHAS TI CHARSAI

یتھ لچّھس تی چرسي

यथ लछस ति चरसुय

Kashmiri Proverb # 100

YETH YE'D TSHHU-NE ZANH TI IWAAN YAD

یہتھ یڈ چّھونہ زھنہ تی عوان یڈ

यथ य़ॅड छॅ न ज़ाह ति यिवान यड

Kashmiri Proverb # 101

ZYADA KASHNAS TSHHE ZYADA RATH

زیاده کشنس،چّھ زیاده رتھ

ज़्याद कशनस छु ज़्याद रथ

* * * * * *

Get in Touch

Dr. Raj Kachru

e-mail: rajkachru@yahoo.com
Mobile: 91-9981549217
303, D.K. Rainbow,
Chuna Bhatti, Kolar Road,
Bhopal-462016, M.P. India

www.ingramcontent.com/pod-product-compliance
Lightning Source LLC
Chambersburg PA
CBHW040748120726
48005CB00012B/1098